managing brand me

WHAT DO YOU STAND FOR?

managing brand me

how to build your personal brand

Thomas Gad
Anette Rosencreutz

www.yourmomentum.com
the stuff that drives you

What is momentum?

Momentum is a completely new publishing philosophy, in print and online, dedicated to giving you more of the information, inspiration and drive to enhance who you are, what you do, and how you do it.

Fusing the changing forces of work, life and technology, momentum will give you the right stuff for a brighter future and set you on the way to being all you can be.

Who needs momentum?

Momentum is for people who want to make things happen in their careers and their lives, who want to work at something they enjoy and that's worthy of their talents and their time. Momentum people have values and principles, and question who they are, what they do, and who for. Wherever they work, they want to feel proud of what they do. And they are hungry for information, stimulation, ideas and answers …

Momentum online

Visit *www.yourmomentum.com* to be part of the talent community. Here you'll find a full listing of current and future books, an archive of articles by momentum authors, sample chapters and self-assessment tools. While you're there, post your work/life questions to our momentum coaches and sign up to receive free newsletters with even more stuff to drive you.

More momentum

If you need more drive for your life, try one of these other momentum titles:

soultrader
personal career strategies for life
Carmel McConnell

reinvent yourself
tactics for work, life and happiness – yours
J. Jonathan Gabay

mental space
how to find clarity in a complex life
J. Jonathan Gabay

be your own career consultant
how to unlock your career potential and help yourself to your future
Gary Pyke and Stuart Neath

coach yourself
make real change in your life
Anthony M. Grant and Jane Greene

change activist
make big things happen fast
Carmel McConnell

lead yourself
be where others will follow
Mick Cope

happy mondays
putting the pleasure back into work
Richard Reeves

innervation
redesign yourself for a smarter future
Guy Browning

the big difference
life works when you choose it
Nicola Phillips

hey you!
pitch to win in an ideas economy
Will Murray

snap, crackle or stop
change your career and create your own destiny
Barbara Quinn

float you
how to capitalize on your talent
Carmel McConnell and Mick Cope

from here to e
equip yourself for a career in the wired economy
Lisa Khoo

grow your personal capital
what you know, who you know and how you use it
Hilarie Owen

PEARSON EDUCATION LIMITED

Head Office:
Edinburgh Gate
Harlow CM20 2JE
Tel: +44 (0)1279 623623
Fax: +44 (0)1279 431059

Website: www.yourmomentum.com

First published in Great Britain in 2002
First ARP Impression 98

ISBN-13: 978-1-843-04017-0

British Library Cataloguing in Publication Data
A CIP catalogue record for this book can be obtained from the British Library.

ARP Impression 98

Cover and concept design by Heat.
Production design by Claire Brodmann Book Designs, Lichfield, Staffs.

Typeset by Northern Phototypesetting Co. Ltd, Bolton

Printed in Great Britain by Clays Ltd, St Ives plc

The Publishers' policy is to use paper manufactured from sustainable forests.

thank you…

We would like to thank Richard Bandler, John Grinder, Steve and Connirae Andreas and Charles Faulkner, who have been our source of NLP techniques. We would like to thank Richard Bandler especially for inspiration and insight into how the human mind works and for his mind-bending sessions.

We would also like to thank Syd Field for the structure of film script writing.

opening

introduction / xv

part one
developing Brand Me

chapter 1
the Brand Me basics / 3

Where does your drive come from? / 4
Make your subconscious mind work for you / 5
The presuppositions of this book / 6
The Universal Communication Model / 9
Real and perceived reality / 15
Transparency and how to handle your sub-personalities / 16
Authenticity is the most important thing in our time / 19
Personal Branding is all about differentiation / 21
How to create a strong personal brand / 22
Go with the flow / 22

chapter 2
the Brand Me method / 25

The stage metaphor / 26
The Brand Me Future Scenario – researching my future / 28
Making my Brand Me Future Scenario / 30
The Brand Me Mind Space – exploring my Functional, Social, Mental and Spiritual Dimensions / 33
The stages of life, or Brand Me over time / 50
The four-dimensional stages of life matrix / 52
How to create my Brand Me Mind Space / 53
The Brand Me Code – what I stand for / 53
Creating my Brand Me Code / 57

part two
integrating Brand Me

chapter 3
installing Brand Me – how to make the change / 67

Personal timeline – an important tool for change / 68
Changing your future – and your past / 69
Discover your personal timeline / 70
Disruption is the key to change / 71
The Brand Me Installer / 72
Taking action and becoming true to your Brand Me / 74
Enhance your charisma – get aligned / 75
The Charisma Controller / 76
Negotiate Brand Me with yourself / 78

chapter 4
packaging Brand Me – now even better / 83

The Brand Me Story – presentation of yourself / 84
Structure the dramatization / 86
Put the story in a dialogue mode / 88
The Brand Me performance – your action on stage/ 89
Pick up your performance / 90

part three
launching Brand Me

chapter 5
activating Brand Me – setting the agenda / 97

Creating your own myth / 98
The myths of IKEA founder Ingvas Kamprad / 99
The Brand Me Activity Generator™ / 100
Speak for yourself / 102
The Brand Me Switch / 104

chapter 6
marketing Brand Me – time for action / 107

Finding the market where your change will make a difference / 109
Why – what are my objectives and targets? / 109
Who is my audience, or my stakeholders? / 110
Choosing your channels / 113
Communicate at your own pace / 114

part four
living Brand Me

chapter 7
job Brand Me – spin off a career / 119

How do you fit the company you work for? And how does it fit you ...? / 122
Matching your brand with the brand of the company / 123
How to choose your career / 127
Find motivation by exploring your Brand Me Code / 131
The Instant Motivator / 132

chapter 8
team Brand Me – join your forces / 137

Team member matching / 138
The team as culture within a culture / 141
The transparent three-level branding system / 142
The Team Brand Workshop / 143

chapter 9
leader Brand Me – go ahead and do it / 149

The five steps to becoming a Brand Me leader / 152
Charismatic leadership advice / 152

chapter 10
relationship Brand Me – make a better match / 159

Partner matching / 161
Relationships over time / 163

part five
future Brand Me

chapter 11
buyer Brand Me – give the right signals in the marketplace / 171

Consumers have always done marketing / 173
Introducing the buyer agent / 174
A new era of branding / 175
A new definition of what branding is all about is needed / 176

chapter 12
real Brand Me – you are one of a kind / 181

The growing importance of being special / 182
What positive lessons can illnesses teach us? / 186
To what extent can you change your body with your mind? / 187
How much of so-called reality can you change with your mind? / 188
The 'body' and 'soul' of the Brand Me Code / 189
Imagine you had another life … / 190
Five keys to the future / 190

closing

further reading / 191

introduction

do you really want to become a brand?

Do you really want to stand in the supermarket of life and be compared to others as if you were a product or package? Imagine being manufactured and standardized like a commodity on the shelf, being compared with 'other brands' on design, looks, image or 'product features'.

Hmmm! Haven't I already experienced that thought? It's not new to me at all, is it?

Was it when someone else won the school prize, or got the job or grant instead of you, or was selected for the football team? Maybe it's those painful memories that make the whole idea of becoming a brand distasteful. Instead we enjoy seeing ourselves as professionals, intellectuals, individuals. Yes, we adapt to the needs of the marketplace, but on our own terms. But maybe it's your revolt against all those times you weren't chosen that motivates you to read this book?

Thinking of me as a brand makes me feel like merchandise, that I'm selling myself, almost prostituting myself.

Thinking of yourself as a brand on the supermarket shelf is of course a shallow and superficial concept, as if it were a question of styling and image alone. Even more, doesn't it also feel soulless and cynical? And commercial? After all, who likes the idea of being sold in the marketplace?

Time to reassure you. In this book, our approach is the exact opposite of soulless and cynical.

Our aim is to help build not only your confidence, but also your dignity in life. It's about clarifying why you are different and unique, what you stand for as a person.

It's true that a lot of us are picked and chosen for different tasks and in different situations, very much on the benefits we are *perceived* to have. And so part of this book is about communicating you to others. But the most important content is concerned with finding out what you stand for, your personal Brand Code. Just as you have a DNA code that determines your physical and mental attributes, your Brand Code determines your values, your qualities and everything you have to offer an employer, a friend, a life partner, your family, etc. The difference is that while you can't do very much about DNA, your Brand Code can be adjusted and modified to communicate you better and to represent the real you.

But isn't branding just the latest jargon? Hasn't branding just become another buzzword for a perceived 'new' kind of marketing? And hasn't marketing just become a fact of life in our times? Does it really offer anything new to the way I project myself in work and life?

The business vocabulary of management, marketing and branding is used as a metaphor to describe and structure personal development for several sound reasons.

Firstly, in the same way that improved branding has been used as a strategic tool to create business success, we believe it can fulfil the same role in your personal success – creating a stronger Brand Me and leading to improved financial, social and mental standing.

Secondly, the vocabulary itself helps you to **enter the right frame of mind for self-management**. In other words it's action oriented and productive and will lead to tangible results. It's less mushy and 'soft' than most popular psychological personal development books, where the language from the outset can be rather offputting to many career people.

Thirdly, **everybody with business experience and business training will relate to the structure and language**. Using a traditional psychology or philosophy structure to describe the same thing would require you to learn and understand the structure first.

Finally, it's **a good modus operandi for working with personal development**; the step-by-step thinking is ideal for handling very complex and subtle issues.

True, the modern concept of a brand (and branding) is trendy and has become something more than just creating a logo and packaging. Branding in its most modern definitions has become a metaphor for all the connected strategy issues that guide a corporation to achieve its goals, and is therefore vital for business success.

The new view is the brand as a non-controversial management tool for leading complex businesses in a very transparent environment, which solves the problem of customer and employee cynicism when it comes to new business ideas. Everyone can use the brand for guidance; it's the DNA code of the company, the Differentiation Code in a business landscape where the similarity, the 'me-too' syndrome, is a major threat.

Ironically, modern branding in business is based on an understanding of human psychology and philosophy.

The 4-D Branding concept for corporations was built on the idea of creating an organic personality, a DNA, in an abstract product or service organization. The approach is to re-create and simulate the mind work of a talented entrepreneur, but within management teams.

The best brands are built by entrepreneurs; and the 4-D Branding method is based on the process by which the entrepreneur identifies what he/she 'stands for' and transfers it to the company and the business. The 4-D concept is to think 'personal' rather than concentrate on a corporate institutional process, building on the fact that every corporation consists of individuals, and that all customers, even business-to-business customers, are in the end individual decision makers.

A talented entrepreneur does this intuitively and automatically. Less communicative entrepreneurs, hired managers perhaps or rather team managers, can use the 4-D Branding method to re-create this intuitive process. So in other words the modern branding of business is all about finding, developing and using the entrepreneurial values in a larger context.

Can't you take me for what I am? Why do I have to change to fit in with your tastes and preference?

The problem with most of us is that we don't know who we are, and we have a very distorted idea of how we are perceived by other people. This book and the methods within it are not about changing personalities – maybe adjusting slightly, but the essence of the book is the old human quest: Know thyself! And the oldest of questions for man: Who am I? Most of the world's philosophical thinking centres on that question.

I don't want to be brainwashed, become like somebody else, like just anybody.

Our intention in this book is just the opposite. It's really about making you different and authentic to yourself. To refine 'what's in me', to find, polish and develop it, to cut yourself like a diamond using the quality of your complex crystallized personality.

We think of ourselves as rather complex, sophisticated, valuable and different. And yet DNA research shows that we are much, much more similar than we like to think we are. The difference between you and any other human on the planet is just 0.05 % of our genetic code. (What's more, we humans are much closer to the chimpanzees than is comfortable for our feeling of superiority, only a 1.6% difference.) How we create real difference is in our expression of our genes and in how we communicate the difference in that expression.

Why personal branding?

- Save personal energy.
- Enhance your charisma.
- Get a transparent core personality.
- Be clear and defined.
- Become respected.
- Be harmonious, balanced … and happy.
- Secure easier, better decisions quickly.

Isn't personal branding very egocentric?

Of course, the focus is on you, so by definition it must be egocentric, but not necessarily egotistic. A person may do things in a very egotistic way all the time, but at the same time be totally unaware of his or her own inner personality. People who are aware of their own selves are better at enjoying relationships with other people. Maybe this has to do with self-confidence. When you know yourself you can lower your guard, and be generous with yourself to others.

It's very philosophical stuff, isn't it?

Personal branding is very much about your mission in life or having your own important issue.

A lot of people don't really bother to think about this very much; they just live their lives. Until one day, struck by a life crisis of some kind, the total perspective, the whole reason for living, suddenly becomes dramatically important.

To create a Brand Me, in the way we suggest in this book, is a very good preparation for any crisis in life. It also gives a certain comfort or peace of mind; you get a good feeling of being complete somehow. The mission in life is not just the 'Mission' part of the Brand Me Code, which we will later introduce you to. It's actually the whole thing, the Brand Me platform, that will help you to fulfil your quest for a mission in life.

If everybody has a personal brand isn't that going to create a very difficult world?

On the contrary, the world is going to become better. It's much more difficult and dangerous if people don't know what they stand for. If you don't have a clear mission or an issue of your own you are in great danger of becoming a victim of fanatics: people with strong personalities and seemingly important missions and exciting issues that at first sound very relevant.

We are so easily seduced by people like that; they usually have the fame, the drive and the differentiation. And most of us are real suckers for an issue: particularly if we don't have an issue of our own we have an urge to import one from someone else. Religious and political leaders know this; they have used this situation for centuries to capture our minds.

Our democracy is actually built on the presupposition that we all know what we stand for and that we are able to match our own ideas about society against the ideas and issues of the people that stand for election to be our representatives in parliament and government, and vote for the ones who fit our own standpoint best. What happens if you don't know what you stand for, and still have to vote on someone to represent you? Well, of course issues that appear attractive in the short term to you will easily seduce you.

This is exactly what happens on the political scene in most countries today. With few exceptions the political parties drive very shallow and short-sighted issues in order to attract people who don't know what they stand for themselves and don't have important issues of their own.

So, personal branding is important for democracy and freedom: a person who knows what he or she stands for is less likely to be vulnerable to anti-democratic charismatic leaders.

The business guru Tom Peters talked about Brand You, while you are saying Brand Me. What's the difference?

People tend to become more and more like brands, and brands for that matter tend to become more and more like people. Commercial brands are becoming value brands, and they are 'standing for something'. But how about people? Isn't it equally important for a person to stand for something? We know that this is true for artists and performers. But in business life also this is becoming more important every day.

Tom Peters pointed this out in his book *Brand You* some years ago, when he showed that the way to make a career in today's network organizations is to 'be somebody' in order to get noticed and be selected for a project team. This book carries on where Tom Peters left off. Moving on from the theory, it deals with the actual creation of your own brand and how to launch it successfully.

The problem with most of us is that we tend to go through life with many different sub-personalities.

We adapt to different situations, pleasing different people in a way that makes life confusing, not only for our many different 'audiences', but also for ourselves. In a more and more transparent world this is becoming a real problem.

To 'stand for' something is crucial in order to become trusted and defined, and to 'stand out' from the crowd is critically important: to get the attention you want, the partner you want, the career you want. It's also vital in order to get the invitations and offers in a consumer-driven market, where intelligent (and soon emotional) agents are shopping around on your behalf.

In today's value-driven network organizations it has become essential to know yourself in order to get the optimal fit between what the organization stands for and what you stand for yourself. At the same time it's necessary for you to communicate what you can contribute to the team: a good team is in effect a blend of different personal brands.

And the reason we called the concept 'Brand Me' is that it's you who are doing the branding: this book is really trying to see everything from your perspective. No one else is telling you who *you* should be, except you yourself.

Are you ready for personal branding?

Personal branding in this way involves defining who you really are, clarifying yourself. Many people don't like this; they prefer to hide. On the other hand, some have a natural talent for defining and communicating what they stand for. They are like talented musicians, playing the music by ear. Some find it more difficult: they need the music written down; they need a process of self-reflection, which for most people will be the introduction to self-development.

The benefit of this process is that you have to explore and express your own view of yourself and how you actually want to be perceived. This is something we seldom do for ourselves; instead we let others describe us.

We almost never think of ourselves in a structured way and very few of us deliberately try to manage and implement our own desired personality systematically.

So, are you really ready for personal branding?

01

chapter one
the Brand Me basics

Where does your drive come from?

Have you ever noticed how much energy you get from doing what really interests you? You can go on for hours and hours without ever getting tired. If you know 'what you stand for' you will do more of the things that motivate you and you will do them better, more effortlessly and with more endurance. It's like getting your energy back.

Our book is all about using this motivating factor, doing more of what you like to do.

The need for this usually appears in crisis situations of some kind: burnout, job loss, divorce. Then you have to deal with these issues urgently. You are in a life crisis and the question: 'Who am I?' becomes really central. Usually you then proceed to accuse yourself of being at fault.

Now imagine that you have been through this difficult situation before. Or in other words, you have asked yourself this question before. You have the answer ready when the situation comes, you are still very much in charge of the situation, and you are on top of things. Think of it as almost a pleasure to confirm things that you already expected, just as mentally well-trained athletes do. The game is an affirmation of what the training has prepared you for.

What will happen is that you might even avoid some of the most traumatic experiences; or at least you'll be prepared to handle the situation much more efficiently.

If you have a strategy to work through, you will be slightly more in control; you will be able to see context, the 'whys' of the situation.

You'll even see some of the negative events as indicators of something positive that will work for your good in the larger perspective.

You will then be emotionally strengthened because you'll know what you stand for, and this will give you a lot of self-respect and strength. This will also impress people around you. In crisis situations they will become less embarrassed and more empowered to support you and help you, whereas a person falling apart before our eyes makes most of us feel awkward and embarrassed, and creates a feeling of helplessness.

Jonathan Gabay, in his book *Re-inventing Yourself* (also in the Momentum series), deals with what you do after the crisis, when you desperately have to find a new life. In this book we would like to prepare you, make you able to go through a crisis without losing control, actually using the crisis to gain momentum without crashing. Martial arts are all about this, going with the power to regain momentum and take command of the situation.

Make your subconscious mind work for you

When you go through the process of finding out what you stand for, right down to your values and deeper attitudes, you realize that most of this content has its origins in the subconscious mind. This may feel uncomfortable for those of us who are not used to travelling in this inner landscape.

That's why we use a strategy and a structured method for finding out what's going on in there and bringing it out into the light, in a controlled way. A lot of this is done by pure insight into what's going on, but a strategy also gives you a possibility to adjust and refine it.

Most of our decisions in life are made quite automatically by our subconscious mind.

There's not much you can do about it consciously. You can't fight your subconscious mind with conscious thought. Your subconscious will always win.

Your chance to change is to put what's in there in another context, or rather to use it to power a new context. For example, you might be working in a company as a controller, and you don't enjoy your work. Your greatest interest and passion is sailing; imagine the power of using your skills instead to manage a large sailing race!

The presuppositions of this book

This book is very much based on the ideas and techniques of NLP. What is NLP? The letters stand for Neuro-Linguistic Programming.

- **Neuro** refers to our nervous system, the mental pathways of our five senses, the way we see, hear, touch, taste and smell.
- **Linguistic** is about our ability to use language and how certain words and phrases mirror our mental images. It's also about our silent language of gestures, postures and habits that reveals our beliefs and thinking.
- **Programming** alludes to computers and suggests that our thoughts, actions and feelings are patterns or habits that can be changed by re-programming or upgrading. You could actually see this whole book like that if you like, as a software upgrade.

Richard Bandler and John Grinder introduced the concept of NLP some 20 years ago, basing it on some ideas that are fundamentally different from traditional psychology. While the latter is primarily concerned with describing mental problems and difficulties, analyzing and categorizing them, and searching back in people's personal history for explanations and causes, NLP is about how our thoughts, actions and feelings work together to form our experience. It's founded on modern thinking in biology, linguistics and information science.

The basis for NLP is a new principle of how the mind/brain works called 'NLP presuppositions'. The general approach is very constructive and very positive: 'People work perfectly'. We may be happy or unhappy at the outcome, but the fact is that certain thoughts, feelings and actions are effectively producing certain specific results. While there is nothing 'wrong' with any of us in the sense of how things are working, we may want to change it. But then we have to change the thoughts, feelings and actions that are producing the result.

The interesting practical difference between NLP and other forms of therapy based on traditional psychology is that it's easy to make the changes: you can do it yourself (obviously, since you have done the original 'programming' in the first place). The only thing you need is to learn the principles of your mind/brain and some suggested simple processes to go with them. It doesn't take months or years of painful and costly therapy to produce results, but rather minutes. And it doesn't hurt. On the contrary a rhetorical question of NLP is: 'How much pleasure can you stand?' (This question is a change creator in itself, since it's disrupting a thinking pattern we have.)

Then the only problem is believing that this could be true, when we are all taught otherwise. For all of us it's tempting to make everything new we hear about into something we already know. If NLP is easy to explain then it can't be new. But NLP really *is* something different, a new view on how the mind/brain and the body are working … together.

It's quick and very efficient, and that is the reason why NLP has got so much attention lately from both professional therapists and also professionals in all kinds of business. NLP is basically about improving communication within yourself and with others, and very well suited for this communicative era of ours.

The NLP presuppositions are:

1. **The map is not the territory.** We tend to respond more to our mental maps (the perceived reality) than to the world itself. Personal Branding is about the perceived reality.

2. **Experience has a structure.** Experiences, thoughts and memories are part of the pattern. If you change the pattern you automatically change your experience. It's thus possible to neutralize our unpleasant experiences and to improve those beneficial to us.

3. **If one person can do something, anyone can learn to do it.** We can take successful people as our role models, and copy their pattern and make it into our own. This is the way we have learned almost everything in life so far. Why think things are impossible before you have tried them when you can get so much mileage from assuming everything is possible?

4. **The mind and body are parts of the same system.** When you change mental patterns it also affects your body systems, your breathing, muscle tension, etc. And the reverse is also true: when you change things in the body system it affects your mind.

5. **People already have all the resources they need.** All the things we talk about in this book everybody has: mental images, inner voices, feelings and sensations. We can use all these resources to improve our life, our thoughts, skills and emotions.

6. **You cannot NOT communicate.** We human beings are constantly in communication. The least of our communication is verbal; most of it is non-verbal. A special body movement, a smile, a certain look in the eye, a tone of voice, a posture, all these are also outer signs communicating inner thoughts.

7. **The meaning of communication is the response you get.** The effect of all communication is what the receiving person perceives it to be, or in other words it has to be filtered through the mental pattern of the receiver. We need to notice how a communication is received in order to change it and make it more effective.

8. **Underlying every behaviour is a positive intention.** It doesn't matter how thoughtless, hurtful or irritating someone's behaviour is, it originally has a positive purpose: people brag in order to be acknowledged, they are aggressive in order to handle fear or hide in order to be safe, for example. Instead of judging that behaviour, we could separate it from the original intent and prepare for the introduction of a new, upgraded, more positive behaviour that would meet the same intent.

9. **People are always making the best choice(s) available to them.** We all have our experience, our personal history, and from that we have formed our strategies. We have learned to do, to think and react in certain ways. From within this pattern we make our choices. That is, until we learn that there are new and better choices available.

10. **If what you are doing isn't working, do something else.** Do anything else. We all have a tendency to do things in the same way we have always done them. The problem with that is that we always get what we have always got. Try something new for a change: there are so many alternatives to almost everything in life.

The Universal Communication Model

This is the basic model of communication and it's the platform for the good communicator. It's the communication skills you need to develop your own brand. You'd better study it carefully. We have made it as simple as possible, but you still may have to read it a couple of times. It's really worth it.

All communication is a non-linear process and starts with trying to make people **understand**. Conscious communication is very much through words and verbal messages. The idea of using language is that you can connect in a meaningful way to people with whom you sometimes don't have a deeper previous relationship. The use of language as a way to match to other people is the essence of communication.

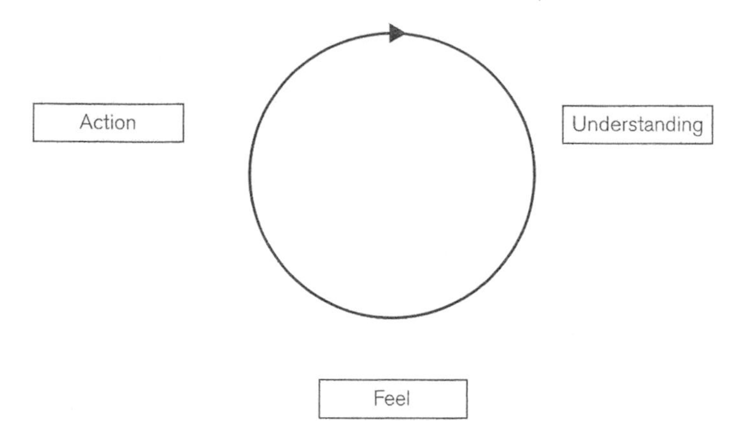

The problem with this knowledge-based structured form of communication is that it almost never produces the outcome that most communication is intended to produce – **action**.

Understanding is usually not enough to produce action. To do that most of us humans have to be motivated: we have to '**feel** for it'. When we don't feel for it, we have no energy to act. Communication is about creating enough mental energy to make us able to act. The amount of energy needed is in proportion to the size of the decision involved in taking action. For example, deciding to buy new toothpaste requires less energy than deciding to vote for Labour when you have always voted Conservative before.

Mental energy is needed to enable any action.

If I don't *feel* like it, I usually don't do it, and if I'm forced to do it anyway, I usually *feel* bad and it colours the whole situation.

In commercial communication we have learned this the hard way. If the customer is not charged with the right feelings, the energy levels will be too low to produce action and a decision to buy. In life it's generally the same thing. You'll need energy to do things. And the way to get that energy is through your emotions. Sometimes just tiny amounts of energy are needed if the task is small. But the larger the undertaking is, the more energy it requires. Energy can easily be lost, for instance in bad relations and in a bad environment (Feng Shui is the traditional Chinese philosophy and methodology for keeping energy levels high in any environment, at home or at work). Life is, simply put, the art of energy balance.

You have to invent and cultivate your sources of energy. Most of the time 'personal energy' comes out of having fun and living a life that is interesting: challenging but pleasant and reasonably secure. Relationships are basically charging situations. Some people will leave you drained of energy (we usually call them energy-suckers) and some people will give you an extra charge that will make your day, week and even life in some few cases. They will charge you with energy to make difficult decisions. If you are that kind of person for other people, you have what we call a very strong Mental Dimension. Maybe you have noticed that those of your friends you feel most relaxed with are those who are giving you energy rather than taking it away.

Back to the Universal Communication Model: *understanding* is never enough to create enough energy for *action*. Even if the logic is there, you need a spark of emotion to act. A lot of communicators get frustrated by this; they don't seem to have this insight, or at least they don't use the insights they have. Governments, officials and big corporations tend to rely on understanding when they communicate. They await action but nothing usually happens. And they get more frustrated, usually to the degree that they speak louder and more powerfully, to enforce understanding by giving the logic, the reasoning for doing one thing or another. Still nothing happens.

A lot of market communicators have spent millions on messages to enhance understanding, all perfectly logical and reasonable. Nothing happens in the market. Or they achieve the opposite of what they wanted. People don't like to be treated as children, or idiots; too much reasoning may be interpreted as 'Do you think I'm stupid, or what?'

The basic idea in *The Cluetrain Manifesto* (the movement and the book by Christopher Locke and Rick Levine) is about the corporate voices, and how totally wrong most of the big corporations are in their communication. As we, thanks to the internet, are entering a one-to-one communication situation, the big corporations are still stuck in the rut of using dominant language, speaking down to people. In our time this a deadly sin: corporations have to be on the same level as their customers, employees and suppliers, and the rest of society for that matter, and to show empathy for people's situation. The same is true for governments, who always seem to take legal texts as their starting point. But in the days of a 24-hour e-government on the web, they will have to adjust the voice and their messages to the new intimacy in communication.

Successful communicators know how all communication has to dip into *feel*, the area of emotions, to charge enough energy to inspire *action*.

When action is taken, it usually means response in some form, wanting to know more; it is at this point that the facts of *understanding* are really important to make the communication process flow. Today the internet gives us the perfect tool for action and response, and we can and will use it to get facts. Surfing is definitely a feel-driven activity, random to start with but usually getting more and more structured.

Passionate people, those who create a lot of interest among others, do create a lot of energy for action, but also a high demand for facts and information about themselves. This is worth thinking about. Usually people of this passionate, emotional nature are very bad at giving facts, information and follow-up on themselves. For example after a presentation they omit to leave behind a CV or something else for deeper study and confirmation of the emotional impression. This is dangerous. The whole idea is to make your communication process complete and not to forget any part of it.

And the other way around, it doesn't matter how much you give out of yourself in information and facts, *understanding,* if you are not able to make it come alive using *feel,* having a personality, giving of yourself emotionally. This is maybe life's most cruel paradox: the more information you have to give, the less people tend to listen.

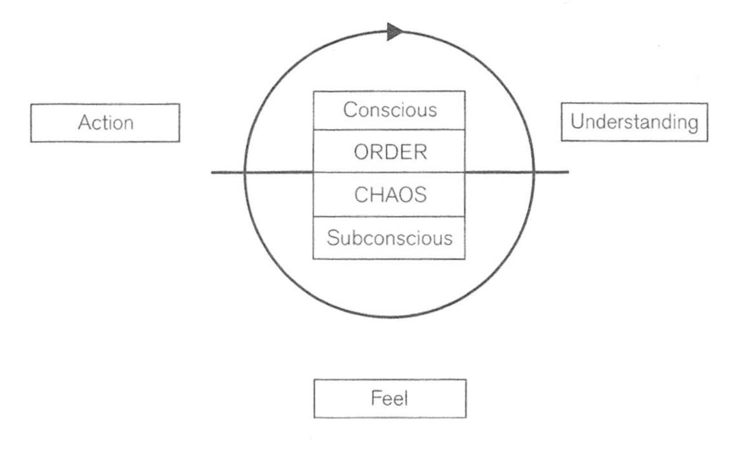

And this can make knowledgeable people very frustrated. They seem to say to themselves, 'If people would just listen to me, they would notice how interesting I am.'

All this boils down to the question of **charisma**, which is so useful for selling, presenting, persuading, leading and making things happen. And the question, of course, is: do you have it or not? Is it a pure talent? Or can one actually achieve charisma?

Our answer is that everybody can, in his or her own way. And there are as many versions of successful charisma as there are charismatic individuals.

To become a successful communicator (and a charismatic one) you need to familiarize yourself with the world of images, symbols and signals. Also basically to accept the state of chaos and feel comfortable with it. Man will always strive for order, that's our nature. But those who feel at home in the artistic, illogical, unstructured and scattered world of chaos will have a great chance of becoming good communicators. Here's a little test. On a scale of one to ten (ten being 'very'), how comfortable do you feel spending a whole evening talking with your friends about something that is completely without meaning in the functional sense, leading to no practical outcome? If you have less than ten on the scale on this one, you might need to open up your mind with some artistic experience, such as painting or writing poetry. Then you are welcome back!

To be able to lose control for a while, experiment, take chances, and let things come to you by their own power is important for the good communicator.

And it's also necessary if you want to communicate with your inner self. Once you have worked through the Brand Me process you have programmed your subconscious mind and you can rely on it to guide you. Then you can allow yourself to embrace chaos and even enjoy it without fears. The guidance from within will keep you on the right road at all times.

Thinking about the concept of selective perception is a good way to check this model's validity. Your reality is perceived through your emotions, filtered by what's top of your mind for the moment and how you are pre-programmed through upbringing and education.

For example a pregnant woman sees prams all over the place, whereas another woman wouldn't see them at all, even if she went to all the same places. She might, on the other hand, see all the young men hanging around. This basic knowledge about how we perceive things differently teaches us the important lesson of filters in our perception and how these are usually subconscious. It's the same with the way we act: we do it subconsciously to a large degree, but we also do a lot of activities in a very conscious way.

Thus if you want to change your life, or at least how you are perceived, you can't simply *understand* what's wrong and then go on to *act* in order to change your behaviour, even if this may work in very defined situations. You may be able to focus your conscious mind to change certain behaviour, but as soon as you are distracted your mind will fall back to its program and you will repeat the same mistake again and again.

The way forward is to communicate more deeply with yourself and *feel* the change by accessing your full subconscious potential.

Real and perceived reality

The question of real reality versus perceived reality gets you deep into the philosophical mire.

Some philosophers, such as the German Immanuel Kant, have claimed that there is only a personally perceived reality. Kant reasoned that we all perceive a table, for example, in very different ways; we have only learned to describe it in a similar way. If the table is made of wood and we knock on it, the sound that is produced sounds different in each individual's ears and mind; the feeling of its surface is also perceived differently, and so on.

Based on that, Kant claimed that there might be an objective reality – *Das Ding an sich* – but it would never be perceived in exactly the same way by any two human beings. In everyday life this would definitely be impractical. Who, for instance, would want to be the owner of physical items in a world with no objective reality? Probably no one …

In a practical life you may want to have something called a 'real' reality. But forget it when thinking about branding and doing something with your own personality. Every time you think about what you 'really' are, or 'really' want, be aware, you can be almost sure it's not perceived the same by others, otherwise it wouldn't be a big thing for you.

We all of us sometimes feel misunderstood, and we probably often are! The best way to counter this is to ensure that you have just *one* reality for people to perceive.

All perceptions are filtered through our personally programmed subconscious filters. Thus everything we see, hear, feel and smell, etc. is our version of 'reality'.

In other words, it doesn't matter how good you are at making yourself clear to others, different people will still interpret you differently. But it helps to be aware of your own filters, the ones you use to filter your 'reality'. Let's assume your filter is Match/Mismatch. This means that when you judge something you are looking to see whether it matches something else in your experience, or not. 'I like this person, because this person's style matches my style.' If you think like this, most of your decisions and your thinking will be based on the perception of matching.

Transparency and how to handle your sub-personalities

In the last few decades Western society has become dramatically much more open.

The thing that's driving this change to openness more than anything is the ease with which information now travels. Of course the internet is instrumental here, but there's actually more to it than that. The technology is accompanied by a change in attitude.

Today the media (and thus people in general) seem to have a greater interest than ever in finding out things about people, politics and businesses that are fishy or unethical. And in countries like France, where public secrets have been institutionalized and respected, sometimes even covered up by the system itself, the media are now demanding the truth and the whole truth.

The truth has become a virtue itself, actually one of our strongest values in the modern Western world. It doesn't matter how big or small the lie, or for that matter the issue itself, or if it's just a missing detail of memory or a slip of the tongue; when the truth is violated it's a crime – at least in the public domain.

Sometimes one can feel that this is totally out of proportion. It seems enough these days just to be accused of something for you to have to resign from your post, like Peter Mandelson, the former minister for

Northern Ireland in Tony Blair's government. Even if your innocence is proved later, as happened to Mr Mandelson and many others in the same situation, and whether this proof comes through an investigation or in a court of law it doesn't matter, the harm is already done.

In Sweden there has been open government for a century or so, 'the open-to-public principle'. That's why Sweden found it hard to go backwards when joining the European Union, where the governmental style still bore traces of southern European governmental confidentiality. It seems this is now changing in the EU also; it simply has to. It will become a citizen's right to have access to all public information in a helpful and non-obstructive way.

Basically the same thing goes for most of us in our private lives as well.

Transparency is not just a trend in politics and business: our private ethics have changed, supported by the new openness that technology provides.

The simplest lie to your boss or your colleagues might surf up when it's least convenient and throw you around. It's not the importance or relevance of the lie that matters; it's the fact that you lied and thought you'd get away with it that disturbs people.

To live the life of a chameleon, to have sub-personalities, will become impossible. In the transparent society in which we live we need to have *one* personality, not many different ones. In the old days we could be one person at work, one person at home and a third person among our friends at the club: no longer!

The problem with sub-personalities, conscious or subconscious, is that they tend to run your life. They consume so much energy: you have to remember what you've said and done when wearing your other hats. The personalities need to be organized and kept intact, and they confuse all your friends, family and other stakeholders.

A person may have the same problem as a company: one part doesn't know what the other is doing, confusing stakeholders with different messages. There doesn't seem to be one single overarching idea in the company, or at least not one single message. The different parts of the company, like your different personalities, don't stand for the same thing.

Even if you have been good up to now in matching a special personality to a special group of stakeholders, one of these days you are bound to screw up. It might be through a mistake on your part, or through the fact that someone in one group of stakeholders just turns up on the wrong occasion, among another group of stakeholders. Say a client of yours unexpectedly turns up as one of your children's friends' parents at school, and sees you acting totally differently as a parent from how you act as a businessperson. It can be charming, but it can also be awkward.

There is a great need for authenticity. The reason for this is that almost everything can be faked.

Products fake. Brands fake. And people fake. The great problem has been: who to trust? Later in this book there is a chapter on how the new genetic discoveries make it possible also to fake, or copy, the Physical You (see Chapter 12). Soon scientists will be able to make a clone of your DNA and create a body double. In a world like that we humans will of course become almost paranoid about everything unique, different and authentic.

The reason why a person has many sub-personalities is that there has been very little effort made by most people to really think about what they stand for in the core of their personality. Instead many of us have opportunistically adjusted ourselves to suit different people and situations in our lives, beginning with our parents, but then carrying on, like a child, to adapt to everybody else in the rest of our lives too.

Authorities of different kinds have even supported this behaviour. In her book *Branding Yourself* Mary Spillane even promotes the concept of people as chameleons, although she warns you against being a charlatan. This is exactly the problem: how do you know when you are being a charlatan and when you are being yourself?

If you just have *one* personality your life becomes much more efficient.

Authenticity is the most important thing in our time

The only really important thing in this transparent world of ours is authenticity – to really be what you are!

There is simply nowhere to hide, no curtain to stand behind, no back-office to escape into. And in today's marketing we emphasize the one-to-one relationship with the customer. Every contact a company has with the customer is a part of the company's marketing. Even the people who produce the invoices are part of the customer relations process or the marketing; at the very least they are part of the after-sales process.

No one today can say 'I don't count for the customers'; the external members of an organization are dependent on the internal organizational support they get. In a service-oriented business that support can have a dramatic impact on the business's success. In a lot of service businesses, for example telecoms, the invoice and technical support may be the only contacts we have with that company. If some of these contacts screw up, as customers we might end up in what is called in all types of subscription business 'churn', customers who drop off and accept an offer from a competitor instead.

Study very good established actors, how they act in different roles. They interpret every role they take on based on their own personality; it is this profoundness and authenticity that make these actors so good and charismatic. It's only the supporting actors who are often different in different roles in order to get a role in the first place. The established actor gets the role for his or her personality; they even get their roles specially scripted for them.

The really good actor has a strong enough personality to use all the time – a powerful Brand Me. This might seem unfair to the actor who really tries to adapt to the role, and indeed for many supporting roles in films or in theatre this support is fundamental. Without the supporting actor's ability to adapt to a certain character, the lead actor would have nothing to contrast to and wouldn't be able to play out their role fully.

These are your options: do you want to go through life as a permanent support actor, playing your sub-personalities like a chameleon as you adapt to situations and other people? Or will you decide to be a lead actor and become a Brand?

What will make the difference will be your ability to develop a strong, consistent self that will radiate charisma and authenticity.

When you have got your personal act together, the styling part will become much easier and more self-evident and natural to live. We like to promote a natural way of living instead of a made-up one!

But even more important … a true personality has to be intuitive. You have to use your subconscious mind to make it work as automatically as when you are driving a car; you cannot think of all the traffic rules or consciously calculate and prepare for all different possible scenarios and be conscious of how to act to respond in the right way to different situations.

Many books about personal change are based on conscious driving all the time, following rules and guidelines. We are much more in favour of consciously getting the insight about yourself and then re-programming your inner self, so that you very quickly become intuitional in your new thinking and acting.

Personal Branding is all about differentiation

As we see it, the Brand Me is the Differentiation Code, the personality code equivalent to your body's DNA.

While the genetic DNA is differentiating your body, your physical being, and your abilities to do things and be someone different from others, the Brand Me Code is about how you want to be perceived as somebody different.

Later in the book, we discuss the growing importance of being different not only in terms of genetic code, because this can now be copied, but in terms of personality, in Brand Me Code, the way you want to be perceived as different.

We know from the latest genetic research – the Genome Project – that there are probably 100,000 possibilities in our genetic code that combine together in a certain way to produce the unique body, You.

Basically it's the same thing with Brand Me: it may be hard to find fundamental differences between you and a lot of other people. Differences in personality, that personal brand of yours, consist of a unique combination of many details. It's worth remembering this when you create your Brand Me, in the next chapter of the book.

The reason for establishing the Brand Me Code in the first place is to communicate your differentiation to others. So there is no point in using very special, very private words. Instead it's the combination, or rather crossing, of two generic words that can establish your special positioning. And of course it's usually a matter of the dramatization of this difference: how do you prove to others that you are different?

How to create a strong personal brand

The creation of a strong brand is done in two steps:

- **Differentiation.** It's difficult to be very different. Differentiation is a combination of many details, each of which can be very generic, and it's usually very subtle.
- **Dramatization.** This is all about magnifying the small differences until they are perceived as important enough to make an impression in the minds of other people.

The smaller the *difference*, the more you have to *dramatize*. A very differentiated person who can do things no one else can do, like in his time Uri Geller, who seemed to have magic powers and could make spoons bend themselves, doesn't have to dramatize very much to become a strong brand. Most of us haven't got that kind of differentiation; we have to dramatize a lot more.

Is this a problem? Well, for most of us it's rather difficult to dramatize our small differences. We tend to be embarrassed about ourselves if we exaggerate. To hear oneself repeat the same dramatized story about oneself over and over again makes most of us feel sick after a while. Here you've got to have staying power. Most of us will change a winning story just because we are tired of it, just as most marketing people tend to get tired of the advertising of their brands long before the audience does. But in fact it's when you feel really sick and tired of your own story that it is taking off in the minds of other people.

Go with the flow

One of our favourite metaphors is looking at **life as a river in which you are swimming** – a broad, streaming river that sometimes can get really wild, sometimes dangerous with rapid falls, but also at times offers nice, calm waters, pools of pleasure.

Of course you have two basic choices in life: to swim upstream or downstream.

Swimming upstream may be more challenging; it may also feel safer and more powerful, especially if you are anticipating a fall waiting for you downstream, a fall you fear you're not going to survive. The main risk with swimming upstream, though, is that you could totally exhaust yourself by swimming against the current and finally drown yourself. Some people do choose this strategy anyway; it's one of control, power and challenge.

The other strategy is to 'go with the flow'; swimming downstream means you can save a lot of energy, you can use this energy to move sideways in the river, you can find the still water, the pools of pleasure, you can do the rapids and navigate to avoid the wildest water. This is the strategy of confidence and curiosity.

Personal branding as we see it is all about 'going with the flow', making more of what you already are and doing better what you already do rather than changing yourself totally.

02

chapter two
the Brand Me method

This is the core chapter of the book: the 'How do I do it?' part. Our aim is to make the establishing of yourself as easy and practical as possible. After all, we are only helping you with the process, the content: what is YOU, what you stand for and how you want to be perceived by others, you will have to supply yourself. The more passion you put into it, the more honest you are to yourself, of course the better the result will be.

Our recommendation is that you start by reading this entire chapter, then go back and do your Brand Me Code before you go on to the next chapter.

In the next chapter we will talk about how to 'take your Brand Me to market', how you tell your story – the Brand Me Story. We will also help you analyze your stakeholders and will help you to choose media channels to communicate and create activities for your marketing plan.

The stage metaphor

The best metaphor for really understanding how to establish your Brand Me is to visualize a theatre.

Or, as William Shakespeare puts it in *As You Like It*:

All the world's a stage,
And all the men and women merely players.
They have their exits and their entrances,
And one man in his time plays many parts,
His acts being seven ages.

A theatre consists of three basic elements:

- The stage itself, on which you stand expressing yourself.
- The audience with a mix of the stakeholders in your life. It's a transparent situation: you have to address them all at the same time.
- The backdrop, the back of the stage where you can have different backgrounds installed. We call this background a scenario, and in the branding metaphor the background is the future into which you want your personality to integrate.

The Brand Me method consists of three basic parts:

- Brand Me Future Scenario
- Brand Me Mind Space
- Brand Me Code.

The **Brand Me Future Scenario** will help you to sort out what scenarios you hold as a **background** to your own brand. This is fundamentally what many people do when they choose a career path, trying to figure out where the best possibilities in the job market will arise. The problem is that you don't usually do this in a structured and profound way.

The **Brand Me Mind Space** describes the perception of YOU in the minds of other people expressed in four dimensions: functional, social, mental and spiritual. There are in reality as many Brand Me Mind Spaces as there are people trying to figure out who you are and what you stand for. When you do it for yourself, though, you work with the transparent situation of a mixed **audience** of stakeholders together in one room and with your desired perception of yourself, i.e. how you'd *like* to be perceived in the minds of other people.

That's why it's such a good idea to do the Brand Me Mind Space before you do the **Brand Me Code**, which is the essence of what *you* finally want to *stand for*.

The **Brand Me Code** in the theatre metaphor is your **script**. You will work on your script and then leave it to your subconscious mind to interpret it, much as a scriptwriter would do, the subconscious mind then being the actor within you that helps you to act it out. Detailed instructions about how to act will never work, just some general ideas from the director.

If you want to be perceived as an authentic and charismatic person worthy of great respect you will have to trust your subconscious mind, the same way you trust it to handle complicated situations like driving a car, or regulating your oxygen intake while climbing a staircase.

But it is a great help for your subconscious mind to have a good script. If you haven't thought about what you stand for, your subconscious mind will use your previous experience as references, and sometimes the result will be something you are not at all happy with.

The Brand Me Future Scenario – researching my future

Scenario planning is an everyday activity for most of us, even if we are seldom aware of it. A healthy mind does scenario planning all the time. We collect and interpret signals in our environment and assemble them into meaningful patterns of development.

Scenario planning is a powerful tool for two important reasons. Firstly, it's an efficient way to understand the logic of change: it helps us to visualize the drivers, the key factors and the key actors and our own ability to influence things. Secondly, it's an efficient planning device, helping us to sharpen our personal branding strategy, to prepare for the unexpected and to watch out in the right direction, monitoring the right issues.

But is it really possible to know what the future of your Brand Me will look like? Of course not! We are not trying to forecast the development when developing the different scenarios. There is a big distinction between scenarios and forecasts. The scenario is different by virtue of the fact that it doesn't want to hide risks. Instead, by using the scenario tool we are able to find and explore the risks.

The model we use for Brand Me Future Scenarios is a very accepted and simple one, but nevertheless effective: it's called 'cross-impact analysis', and is very valuable if you want a more detailed and refined picture of your own future. In the new worlds of opportunity at the crossroads of two trends, a totally new profession or opportunity for a business or a future life can arise, as happened when the healthfood and ecological trends combined. We will describe exactly how you handle this below.

On what horizon should you plan your Brand Me? Five years? Ten? Fifteen? Or longer?

We recommend that you have a five- to ten-year planning cycle for your Brand Me. After five years you can sit down and revise your Brand Me for the next five to ten years. After all, five years is a long time in a world that seems to change ever faster, and, even if it may be illusory to do so, it's good to look at life like a project.

When you do this planning, also consider what lifecycle you are in. The lifecycles run in seven-year intervals and it's very important to consider what's important for you in your present lifecycle and the one to come.

Making my Brand Me Future Scenario

We recommend you do this particular workshop together with somebody else. Since this is about the background of your Brand Me Code and not the code itself it's fine to share and discuss alternative views on the future. You don't necessarily have to agree; on the contrary, different views of what the future holds will benefit the process, as you will see below. And after all, who knows exactly what the future will be like anyway?

STEP ONE

Our method for creating a Brand Me Future Scenario begins with collecting information about trends, forecasts and future predictions that's relevant to your Brand Me.

You can do this from various sources, preferably using the internet. Search for trends in the areas you perceive as relevant or interesting to you. There are loads of trend forecasters; they all have their own newsletters and write articles. The leading trade magazines in your trade or line of business are also good sources; most of them are on the net. But most of all you should rely on the material that you already have in your own memory.

STEP TWO

Out of this material on future trends you are looking for background factors and key variables.

The **background factors** are statements about the future that are general enough to be able to be a part of all scenarios. They might be things like 'the market economy will be maintained', or 'technological development will proceed as now for the next five- to ten-year period'.

Two important assumptions should govern the background factors:

- **Continuity.** No catastrophes will happen during the planning time, neither natural catastrophes, nor social revolutions or the equivalent. The world may be a more dangerous place these days but if you try to factor in the totally unpredictable you will get nowhere in your planning.
- **Human beings will not change.** Evolution will not be able to change the basic present nature of us humans in our lifetime; it will take time before genetic engineering will affect us. We expect that our basic needs of food, sleep, etc. will not change, and that our priorities in other areas will remain the same.

With **key variables**, or major trends, we define factors or dimensions that are likely to have great impact on your Brand Me, but are more or less uncertain; we really don't know how they might develop.

When we look at key variables we are not interested in more or less certain developments. So, for every key variable we describe at least two different directions in which things might go. Here you can profit from having a different opinion from someone else about how things will develop!

A key variable can be, for example, place of work, with distance working or home working at one end of the spectrum and working in an office at the other. This trend might affect both your life and your Brand Me.

STEP THREE

Now it's time to map together the alternative development of key variables; this is the cross-impact analysis we mentioned earlier. Crossing two variables gives you four possible scenarios. Keep on creating as many scenarios as you think are meaningful; we call these 'My New Worlds'.

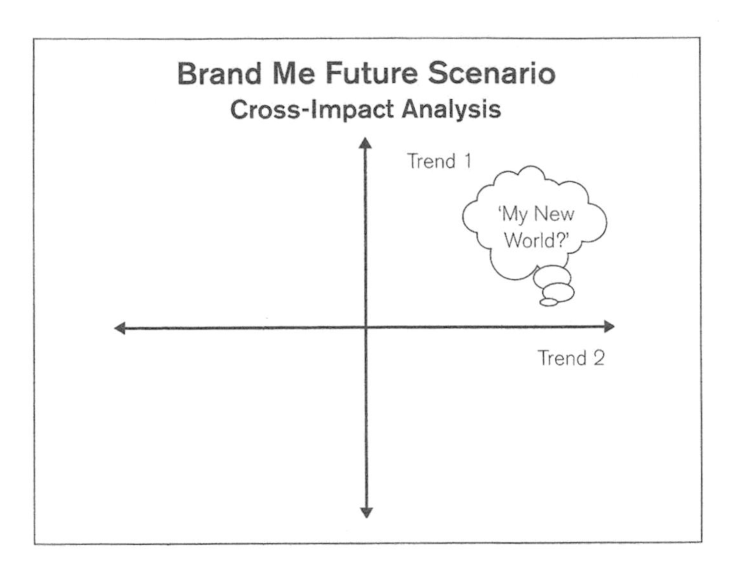

STEP FOUR

Finally it's time to choose the one scenario above all others to use as the backdrop of the stage on your Brand Me theatre – the Brand Me Future Scenario itself.

Sometimes it's difficult to choose just one scenario, but it's much more difficult to work simultaneously with two or more, and keep them clear and distinct in your mind when you later come to match your Brand Me Code to them and try to judge how good the match and the possible outcome would be. Try to make a serious effort to choose what you believe is your most probable Brand Me Future Scenario.

STEP FIVE

If you like, you can describe and document the chosen New World in your Brand Me Future Scenario in detail. We sometimes make a mood-board of it, a scrap board with articles, headlines, visuals, etc. cut out from newspapers and magazines. This helps to create a clear image for yourself of your expected scenario.

The Brand Me Mind Space – exploring my Functional, Social, Mental and Spiritual Dimensions

Our leading idea of personal branding has its foundation in this four-dimensional model, which in its turn is based on the idea of the brand as something that is taking up space in other people's minds; hence the term Brand Me Mind Space.

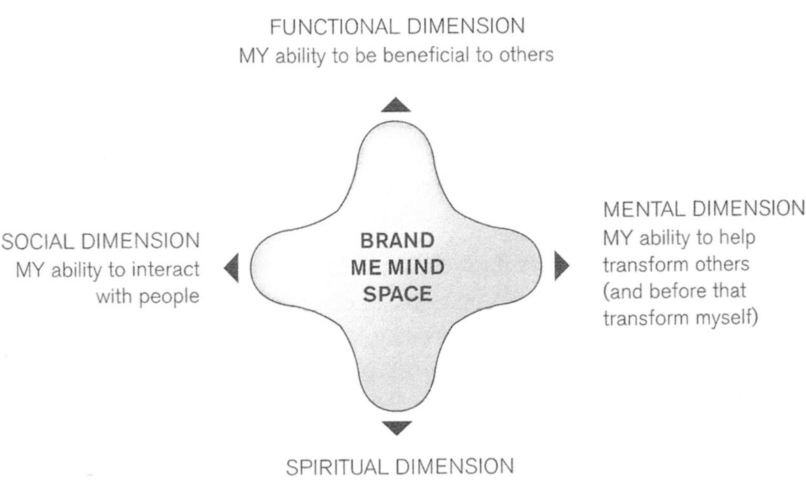
FUNCTIONAL DIMENSION
MY ability to be beneficial to others
SOCIAL DIMENSION
MY ability to interact with people
BRAND ME MIND SPACE
MENTAL DIMENSION
MY ability to help transform others (and before that transform myself)
SPIRITUAL DIMENSION
MY ability to spiritually connect to totality in life, and take on local or global responsibility for ecology, ethics, an issue, etc.

Think back on all those people who have made a big impression on you; they don't necessarily have to come from the public sphere. The one thing they will probably have in common is that they take up a lot of your mind space.

The Brand Me idea is about exactly how to make that happen in other people's minds, it's about how you will be able to stretch out your Brand Me Mind Space as far as possible.

To do this you usually have to use more than one dimension. Of course there are people who are very strong in one dimension and who are able to take up a lot of space only because this one dimension is so large. In public life in particular a one-dimensional

Brand Me Mind Space is very common. An athlete typically becomes famous for a special talent in one dimension (usually the functional), like Tiger Woods in golf.

To become a strong brand with staying power takes more dimensions.

A full 4-D personality creates a stronger persona over time

Throughout the book you will find diagrams like the one above with a public person's persona mapped in the four dimensions (in accordance with the 4-D Brand Me Mind Space model).

There are two reasons for including public personas like this. One is to show how the model can be used to quickly map how you perceive another person's personality, which can be very helpful for you in many situations in private life and in business.

There is also another reason, and that is to give some examples of role models, modelling a complete 4-D personality in some cases, or particular strengths in some of the dimensions in others.

Since role modelling is such an important tool for change and development (as it has been for all of us since childhood) these examples are of course not enough and not exactly the ones you would prefer, but they might give you a pattern and inspiration for analyzing other role models more suitable for your purposes.

The Functional Dimension dominates with public personas, but they have a lot to gain in stretching their brands.

International actors and models get a lot of public attention and they are able to gradually express their multidimensional personalities. Some are probably doing this intuitively; others may have advisers.

By doing this they strengthen their public persona continuously and tend to take up more of our mind space and become more valuable for directors, producers and film and TV studios. Their income, of course, increases and that is one of the drivers for them to work on the completion of their personality.

For the rest of us, not being media personalities, our direct income might not be affected by doing the same. But indirectly we make ourselves useful, needed and appreciated much more if we build multidimensional 'Mind Spaces' of ourselves in other people's minds. More people than ever in business life are taking on a personal coach in order to get individual inner support and a stronger presence in the public domain.

On what criteria have we chosen our examples? Well, we wanted to represent different areas – sport, entertainment, culture, politics and business – and we also wanted personas of both sexes. We have also chosen people who have been out there for a while as public personas, thereby avoiding the latest and trendiest people, because it simply takes time to build a brand, especially a consistent 4-D brand.

Coco Chanel

One of the oldest and strongest corporate and product brands based on a strong personal brand and entrepreneur serves as a good introduction to the Brand Me Mind Space for public persons.

Keeping to her motto, 'In order to be irreplaceable one must always be different', Coco Chanel has definitely made her mark in history, not only as probably the most influential and innovative fashion designer in modern times, but also as a role model and inspiration for women. She had a strong Spiritual Dimension: the liberation of women played an important part in her work. Raised by nuns in a French orphanage, she travelled through society guided by her stated wish to be different. And she was.

Having a strong Mental and Spiritual Dimension she dramatized this fact rather than trying to assimilate when being introduced into new social contexts. First out of necessity. She couldn't afford the fashionable clothes of the period, so she rejected them and made her own, using simpler, affordable, everyday materials. She invented her own style influenced by the style and fabrics of men's wear: sports jackets and ties, etc. These cleaner, more comfortable cuts introduced to women's wear came to be her trademark. Combined with fake jewellery, which she introduced and which made 'jewellery' accessible for more women, a new style was born.

Coco Chanel Brand Me Mind Space

FUNCTIONAL DIMENSION
She was a leading designer and introduced the 'little black dress' and suit for women, as well as the cheaper bijouterie to allow many women to wear 'jewellery'
SOCIAL DIMENSION
She kept a rich social roster with artists, politicians and business people
BRAND ME MIND SPACE
MENTAL DIMENSION
Her ideas and inspiration are still alive; she was unconventional, never marrying, keeping lovers
SPIRITUAL DIMENSION
She helped to liberate women and make their lives easier, changed values and made women more equal to men

Her breakthrough came in the 1920s, and this transformation of style during the 1920s and 1930s played an important part for women in expressing their freedom.

Never marrying, Coco Chanel kept her independence and had various lovers (who helped her finance her business at the outset). But she almost got married once; it was to one of the richest men in Europe, the Duke of Westminster. When she didn't, her explanation was, 'There have been several Duchesses of Westminster, but only one Coco Chanel'.

The strong ideas and values behind her brand and style made a comeback possible in the 1950s, despite the fact that her reputation had greatly suffered as the result of a love affair with a German Nazi officer during World War II. The style was revived and refined, in particular her timeless suits. By the late 1960s, Chanel had become part of what she once rebelled against – the Establishment. When the topic was brought up she responded by saying, 'Fashion is not simply a matter of clothes. One intuits it.'

A lot of public people are well known for their Functional Dimension, for being excellent authors, painters, musicians, scientists and politicians, etc., and are better known for their work or their ventures than for their personalities, that is insofar as we can tell from their public personas.

In their private life they might be much more of a multidimensional personality than in their public life. And that's all very well. But the problem is that if you tend to be well known for what you do rather than for what you are, you automatically become more vulnerable if your work goes out of fashion or you drop out of the public spotlight. If you are then less of a personality you are simply easier to forget or to neglect.

If you, on the other hand, become a complete 4-D person you will touch people's minds in so many ways that you'll stay there, taking up a lot of mind space, even if your dominant dimension becomes less important.

Stretching the perception of your Brand Me

The Brand Me Mind Space is like one of those jelly-formed slimes that you can stretch out in different directions, and which if you let go, will shrink and return to its original form. In theory, this is also the case with your Brand Me: if you don't stretch it all the time it will in time disintegrate and vanish, become a forgotten or at least a passive entity in other people's minds.

When we studied commercial corporate brands we found out that successful brands had the ability to stretch out beyond relevance in the minds of consumers.

A good example is Apple Macintosh, which takes up a lot of space in people's minds, much more than most PC brands, despite the fact that Apple Macs have little relevance as a product to most people because of their proprietary operating system and their niche marketing towards graphics and design users.

It's the same thing with individuals. There are a lot of people who may have real relevance to you in your life, but you still don't regard them as terribly important to you. Whereas there may be others who have very little relevance, but they nevertheless mean a lot more to you, as mental role models or as a social centre for your life, etc.

Our four-dimensional Brand Me Mind Space idea came about when we studied the Brand Mind Space of commercial brands, what made them so strong, and found out that their activities and effect on the audience could be clustered into four different categories. These categories later became the four dimensions of the Brand Mind Space of the brand. And now we have found that this four-dimensional model is very productive when working with your personal brand as well.

The 4-D Brand Me Model simplifies the complexity of a person; it sees the person as one entity but with many dimensions ranging from the physical, materialistic, earthbound, and social to the holistic mental, with a spiritual connection with eternity. In different parts of your lifecycle different dimensions play different roles.

Functional Dimension

This may be the part of your personal brand that is the most traditional part of yourself. It's usually about more or less tangible skills, and definitely about your ability to **produce benefit to others**, to your family, your partner in life, your company, and your employees if you are the entrepreneur, and so on.

The Functional Dimension answers the question: how can you be beneficial to yourself and to others?

And of course, this means how you can be **perceived to be beneficial**, not necessarily what good you actually do.

Björn Borg

Björn Borg is one of the most talented tennis players in the history of tennis; of course he has a gigantic Functional Dimension, totally unrivalled in number of Wimbledon victories, etc. In the Mental Dimension he had a lot of influence during his active years on a younger generation of tennis players, like Mats Wilander and Stefan Edberg. In the Social Dimension he comes across as a very shy person, and in the Spiritual Dimension he hasn't shown passion for any causes outside of tennis. His Functional Dimension is clearly the one he became famous for.

Björn Borg Brand Me Mind Space

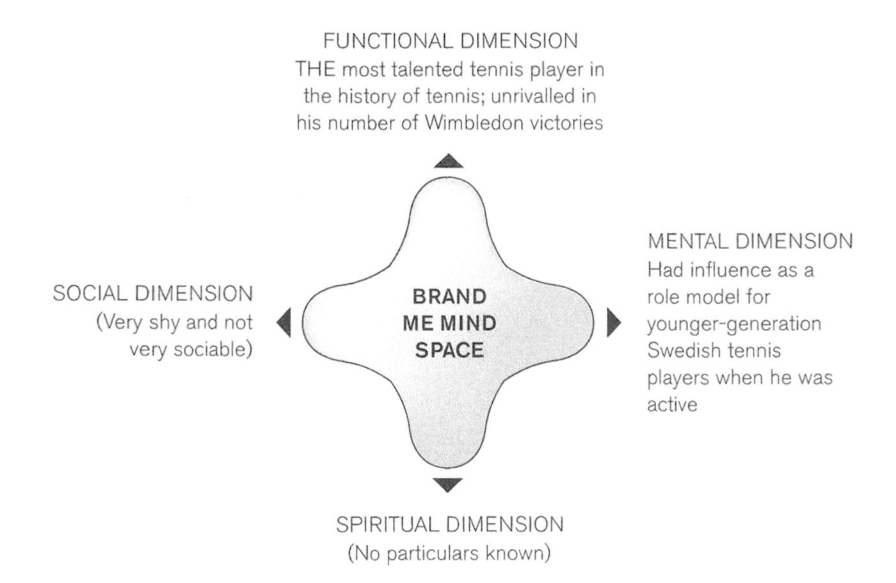

FUNCTIONAL DIMENSION
THE most talented tennis player in the history of tennis; unrivalled in his number of Wimbledon victories
MENTAL DIMENSION
Had influence as a role model for younger-generation Swedish tennis players when he was active
SOCIAL DIMENSION
(Very shy and not very sociable)
BRAND ME MIND SPACE
SPIRITUAL DIMENSION
(No particulars known)

Remember that we are talking about you as a brand here, the perceived reality, not necessarily the real reality of what you actually are and do.

You may feel that you have many hidden strengths in your personality, but if you are not able to communicate that picture of you, from a personal branding point of view, those strengths are non-existent.

The functional side of your perceived personality has to do with your professional and formal abilities or skills. These can, of course, be based on your education and formal training. But they can also be the result of your experiences.

A favourite word for the Functional Dimension of a person is **competence**, a nice fruity blend of knowledge and experience. The Functional Dimension is also about **productivity** in economic terms. What's your product, how can you be beneficial to a company, a partner or a friend?

The Functional Dimension is about your **deliverables** as a person, mainly in your work life but equally so in other areas of activity, such as you as a brand in your golf club, or in your family or in any other organization. Not the social aspect here, but the functional.

A typical expression of the Functional Dimension could be: 'Thomas is such a good analytical thinker, and such a good presenter of very complex issues.'

People with a very clear and strong Functional Dimension include professionals such as lawyers, doctors and specialists in IT, people who are clearly valuable for everybody on a personal or corporate level.

Social Dimension

In personal branding the Social Dimension is about your **social skills**, your ability to **relate** to other people. It's also about what makes you attractive enough for other people to want to relate to, and about your talent to **organize and lead** people.

The clearest indicator that you have a strong Social Dimension is if you are someone whose name other people might drop.

The extremely successful person with **charisma** is, like a good corporate brand, able to create a 'cult'. A popular word for the Social Dimension is leadership, but leadership is more complex than that – a good leader must have Functional and Mental Dimensions as well.

To have a strong Social Dimension is to be a **naturally sociable** person: a person who is invited sometimes just to make other people feel good, a funny, amiable or interesting character, someone admired by others.

Sir Richard Branson

The corporate brand of his company is Virgin, but Sir Richard Branson has become almost synonymous with it. Branson is a living symbol of the whole Virgin empire, demonstrating how a brand with strong, almost personal values can stretch itself from records to airlines, cola, bridal wear, internet services and personal savings. So, looking at Branson as a personal brand is a lot like looking at Virgin as a corporate brand.

The Functional Dimension of Branson is the one of a real entrepreneur with an instinct for every business opportunity and a sense of entertainment.

His Social Dimension is probably his most developed dimension as a personal brand. As a charismatic leader he has a great talent for making things happen and for making other people enthusiastic and able to teamwork.

Branson's Mental Dimension is in being a role model for entrepreneurs in their fight with established and oblivious corporations; he demonstrates courage and the drive for change and the exploration of new possibilities. His around-the-world ballooning adventures are great metaphors for the lightness and courage he shows challenging established concepts and structures.

His Spiritual Dimension is his dynamic drive to expose the Establishment and promote real deregulation of de facto monopolies, also to make complicated things easier and boring things more fun.

Sir Richard Branson Brand Me Mind Space

FUNCTIONAL DIMENSION
A real entrepreneur with an instinct for every business opportunity and a sense of entertainment
SOCIAL DIMENSION
A charismatic leader with great talent for making things happen, making others enthusiastic and able to teamwork
BRAND ME MIND SPACE
MENTAL DIMENSION
A role model for entrepreneurs in their fight with established and oblivious corporations; demonstrates courage and the drive for change and exploring new possibilities
SPIRITUAL DIMENSION
Exposing the Establishment and promoting real deregulation of de facto monopolies; making complicated things easier and boring things more fun

A typical occupation for a person with a dominant Social Dimension is as team leader in an organization or as salesperson; many people in sales have the talent of being the one that others wait for before they start a meeting ... or a party.

A typical expression of the Social Dimension is: 'Sarah is good fun and caring at the same time.'

Mental Dimension

This dimension is about **developing yourself** mentally, and then as a next step being able to coach others to develop themselves.

It's about being able to **give insights** to people and to help them transform. It's definitely a lot about **inspiring** other people.

The typical personifications of this dimension are the mentor, the teacher, the coach or – at the extreme – the guru.

The Mental Dimension is all about the ability to transform other people, to have them develop personally as a result of contact with you.

The basis for this is that you have been able to transform yourself (maybe as a result of a contact with someone else with a strong Mental Dimension). You will probably have some kind of inner stability, conviction – even **enlightenment**.

John Cleese

John Cleese is an interesting example of how a comedian and actor can expand his Brand Me Mind Space and expand as a personality, becoming much more profound and 'serious' in a good way.

Of course he has a strong Functional Dimension as comedian and actor, but John Cleese, with his creativity and acting in *Monty Python*, *Fawlty Towers*, and so on, is also very much into a Mental Dimension, demonstrating the absurdity of human behaviour and helping us to learn from it.

Recently he has become much more profound in endeavour through his two books about relationships and psychology: *Family* and *Relationships*. In these books John Cleese is asking all the questions that we all want to ask but do not dare to, and he gets them answered in a conversation with a good, experienced psychologist. Without doubt those who have read these books have a much more profound view of John Cleese and much more respect for him and for his ability to share his mental insights and development with others.

John Cleese Brand Me Mind Space

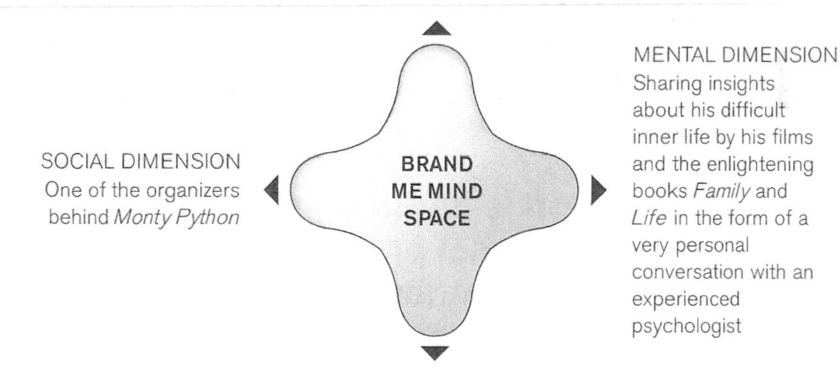

FUNCTIONAL DIMENSION
Brilliant writer, comedian and actor
MENTAL DIMENSION
Sharing insights about his difficult inner life by his films and the enlightening books *Family* and *Life* in the form of a very personal conversation with an experienced psychologist
SOCIAL DIMENSION
One of the organizers behind *Monty Python*
BRAND ME MIND SPACE
SPIRITUAL DIMENSION
Takes on a responsibility in the way he is exploring human nature and psychology based on his personal experience (see Mental Dimension)

To have a strong Mental Dimension in other people's perception means that you have a talent for creating rapport with others, and you most probably show empathy, the ability to put yourself easily into other people's shoes. You are a philosopher of a kind. 'Anette really listens to me and gives me new insights about myself' could be a typical expression of the Mental Dimension.

Typical professional roles for a full Mental Dimensional personal brand include corporate seniors, and all kinds of therapists, consultants and mental trainers. People generally regarded as 'wise', such as some very talented management advisers, could also fall into this category.

Spiritual Dimension

The Spiritual Dimension is about being **connected with totality** in life.

This might sound strange at first, and indeed this is probably the most difficult of the four dimensions to grasp.

Almost all of us are searching for a mission, **a role in society or an issue**. So the fact that some of us instinctively take on a **responsibility** for something larger than ourselves, or even the company or organization we work for, is completely natural, and important for our own self-respect and identity.

The Spiritual Dimension is about serving higher purposes than the traditional professional does. It involves the capacity to contribute to everybody's welfare and to public development at large.

Some people have a talent and a motivation for this. Of course, you can have a profession connected with it, as do social workers, priests, artists and environmentalists. But many people have the capacity to make this sort of contribution within their existing work or as a part of their private life.

Every community, as well as every company, needs these idealists, who are a very important part of the success, mostly because they have a **larger view**; they are visionaries and future-drivers.

Ethics is also an important part of the Spiritual Dimension. This includes respect for life and environmental responsibility for generations to come.

To figure out your potential on the Spiritual Dimension you have to ask yourself what it is in life that gives you the most satisfaction. If the answer is something tied to local or social responsibility, then you have a good Spiritual Dimension to exploit.

An expression of the Spiritual Dimension could also be: 'Steven's passion is to develop a better and simplified IT infrastructure for the benefit of everyone.'

The Spiritual Dimension can also be about **aesthetics**: design, art and beauty. Beauty is philosophically very important for us human beings. The ultimate thing in design is to combine beauty and functionality. The same thing applies to people.

The ultimate person is the one who can combine, for instance, engineering, or scientific skills, with a true sense of beauty.

In many cultures, like the Japanese, this kind of balance between the practical, functional side of things and the poetic and aesthetic has always been highly valued. Historically too this combination in an individual was seen as very important. Leonardo da Vinci, balancing the scientific and the artistic, was an ideal for most educated people of his time. And maybe we will see a rebirth of this Renaissance Man or Woman in our own time.

Sir Bob Geldof

Sir Bob Geldof undoubtedly has a very strong Functional Dimension. Although he has not been tremendously successful at producing hits, which he openly admits, he has a great knowledge of the entertainment world.

In addition to being a musician he is an experienced TV producer and the founder of several production companies like Planet 24 and 10Alps, creating new TV and entertainment ideas.

Lately he has also become a rather successful businessman in the associated field of the leisure industry, being able in the midst of the dot-com crisis profitably to sell his start-up to one of his larger competitors.

Geldof's approach in the travel business is of course based on his own experience in entertainment and as a family man: 'I want to help families book travel easier and make it more fun.' And when he describes his travel business you can trace his passion: he uses words like: 'sexy', 'weird', 'fun', 'good' and 'usable'.

The Social Dimension of Geldof is demonstrated by his great talent for bringing people together for a purpose, in fundraising as well as in business, as an inventive TV and entertainment producer and fundraiser. He is inspirational and a true leader, being able to manage creative people with large egos, which is no easy thing.

Bob Geldof is a role model for a lot of people, some in his immediate vicinity no doubt, but the majority at a distance. He inspires other people to make a difference ('It *does* matter what you do') and he shows how to do it wholeheartedly. Recently he has also shown how you can combine being a good entrepreneur and businessman with having a mission to fulfil.

The great mission of Bob Geldof is helping poor nations and poor people; Band Aid and Live Aid are the best-known examples. But Geldof hasn't stopped there:

he continues to drive forward new issues within this mission, chiefly by lobbying for a write-off of the debts of poor countries. For example he wrote an article in *The Observer* in April 2001 with the message: the G-7 nations cancelled their debt, so why not also the IMF and the World Bank?

As a private person, he also shows he is a man of integrity and responsibility, as demonstrated by the way he provided a safe home for the daughter of his ex-wife Paula Yates and Michael Hutchence, following the suicide of both her parents.

Sir Bob Geldof Brand Me Mind Space

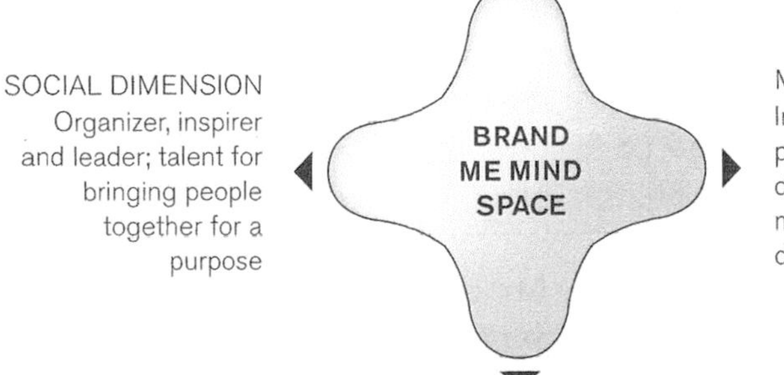
FUNCTIONAL DIMENSION
Musician, charity fundraiser, TV producer and business entrepreneur
SOCIAL DIMENSION
Organizer, inspirer and leader; talent for bringing people together for a purpose
BRAND ME MIND SPACE
MENTAL DIMENSION
Inspiring other people to make a difference ('IT DOES matter what you do')
SPIRITUAL DIMENSION
A great passion for helping poor nations and poor people: Band Aid and Live Aid, and recently the campaign for the write-off of debts of poor countries

The stages of life, or Brand Me over time

How important is your age for the Brand Me process? Of course your age has an important effect on your personality, and, if this is so, is the Brand Me process then of any use at all at certain ages?

These are excellent questions and difficult to answer very simply. One way to clarify the issue is to use a traditional esoteric model of life's stages and apply it to four-dimensional thinking.

You can't take any shortcuts to maturity, and certain parts of the self develop in cycles all through your life.

Being aware of this gives you an insight into yourself and your development over time and how you can make the best of the stage where you are right now.

According to old esoteric teachings life goes in seven-year cycles (7–14–21–28–35–42–49–56–63, etc.). You are beginning your adult life at the age of 21. You start your life task at 28. You are becoming mature to esoteric insights at 35. And so on. We will come back to this later. Rudolf Steiner among others has used these thoughts in his anthroposophic teachings.

In some older literature (for example Shakespeare's *As You Like It*) 'the seven ages of man' are mentioned. In the time of Shakespeare, 49 was considered to be old. Today we may expect if healthy to live beyond 80 years of age, so having ten lifecycles or ages is in order. Above we have alluded to eight, beginning at 21. Obviously there are two more: 7 (when most children go to school) and 14 (when children become adolescents).

Another interesting fact that may support the seven-year-cycle concept is that the human body renews every cell every seven years until the age of about 60.

Before every new stage there is a period during which you unconsciously prepare for the next cycle, usually one to two years beforehand. During this time you typically feel confused about which path to take. This is absolutely natural and a fascinating aspect of life. You are open to new ideas, insights, thoughts and impressions during this period; in fact you are growing as a person. And when you eventually reach the stage itself you'll have made your decision, and will know you are on track for another few years.

Let's take a very general example: at 28 you start studying again or begin a serious relationship, at 35 you may feel like getting married and having your first child, at 42 you break up from an old relationship and start a new one (around 40 is the time for the classic mid-life crisis), at 49 you are at the peak of your career, taking important new steps in personal development, and so on. Go back through your own personal history and remember when you made important changes or came to crucial decisions.

Here are some brief examples of turning points in life for people we know:

- Robert, having tried to make it as a musician, decided that he would go into business after all. At 28 he went to university to take his MBA.
- Eric, at 35, desperately wanted a child with his girlfriend. She became pregnant and they married, even before they had a place big enough for a family.
- Tom remarried at 35, and got a first child, followed by another one three years later. Before that he had been very reluctant to even think about children.
- Peter left his family and divorced at 38. At 42 he moved back in again.

The four-dimensional stages of life matrix

Certain dimensions become more important in certain periods of life. However, you should prepare yourself by establishing a complete Brand Me Mind Space now! If you then look at life from a four-dimensional point of view you will recognize how at different stages in life different dimensions become more relevant. This is exactly how a person usually builds up a Brand Me Mind Space; it's created over time and in steps, and generally as described below.

Age	*Stage*	*Dimension*
21	Beginning adult life	Functional: learning ideas and skills
28	Starting life mission	Social: social context important
35	Maturing to insights	Mental: insights about yourself and your relationships
42	Questioning life	Spiritual: starting to connect holistically
49	Crowning career	Functional: maximizing capacity
56	Mentoring	Mental: coaching others
63	Enjoying life	Social: initiatives to bring people together
70	Searching for origin	Spiritual: insight about role in universe

How to create my Brand Me Mind Space

STEP ONE

Start by asking yourself the following questions:

- 'How am I **beneficial** to myself and to others?' (Functional Dimension)
- 'How do I **relate** to other people and what makes me attractive enough for other people to want to relate to me?' (Social Dimension)
- 'How do I **give insights** to other people, **inspire** them and help them **transform**?' (Mental Dimension)

- ‘How do I **contribute** to everybody’s **welfare** and to **public development**?’ (Spiritual Dimension).

STEP TWO

Make a visual board of your 4-D Brand Me Mind Space, i.e. your preferred perception of yourself, using scrap material from magazines. Cluster the images that you feel represent yourself in each of the four dimensions. You can use several pictures to describe each dimension. Get your inspiration from the answers you gave to the questions in Step 1.

STEP THREE

Now put into words what's on the mood-board. Again use your answers to the questions in Step 1 as support.

STEP FOUR

With the help of friends, research how you are perceived today. You can do this by using the same questions as in Step 1.

STEP FIVE

Compare how you want to be perceived with how you actually are perceived by your friends. Identify the differences and document them; they will be of good use when you do the Brand Me Code later.

The Brand Me Code – what I stand for

The Brand Me Code is for your personality what the DNA code is for your body. It's your Differentiation Code: it will constantly remind you, in a personal way, how you are different from other people.

The difference between the Brand Me Code and the Brand Me Mind Space is that the Mind Space is about how you want to be *perceived* in other people's minds; it's the expected outcome of your personal branding, if you like. The code is the combination of what you actually feel that you *can* and *will* stand for; it's the tool to allow you to achieve your target.

Probably a lot of the content is the same; we certainly encourage you to use the Brand Me Mind Space when doing your Brand Me Code.

Honesty is crucial when you work through this process – what's the point in fooling yourself?

The Brand Me Code has six 'inputs' – Benefit, Positioning, Style, Mission, Vision and Values – and all these are crystallized into your own personal Motto, something to keep in mind as a personal 'mantra' to associate with, and above all to base your personal decisions on.

Let's look at the content of each of the inputs first, and then finally your Motto.

Benefit

'What makes me beneficial to others?'

Looking at yourself as a product or service, you have to ask yourself what is the greatest benefit you bring to others, to your family, your partner in life, your company, your employees if you are the entrepreneur or boss, and so on. This is also about your professional and formal abilities or skills.

An example: ' I'm a good organizer and a responsible husband.'

Positioning

'What makes me different, more competent and/or more talented than others?'

What is it that you do best? This a very essential question in branding – it leads you to explore and express your differentiation.

An example: 'I'm very good at making people laugh; at the same time I'm a very respected leader.'

Style

'What characterizes my style, my image, behaviour, tonality, etc.?'

When we talk about style, we mean the perception that you create – or want to create. It is more about the direct impression you make, your attitude and the feelings you create among others, whereas your deeper personality lies in your values.

An example: 'My style is low-key and trustworthy. I listen more than I speak.'

Mission

'What is my role in society, my issue, my larger responsibility or my passion in life?'

The mission is about purpose, or your benefit to the community. It's what you do, or would do, without getting paid for it. Don't be afraid to scale up your thing to a level where it is important for mankind or at least the local community.

An example: 'My role in life is to develop ways for people to use their power to become better buyers.'

Another example: 'My passion is to promote fine wines in order to cultivate people's senses and make them enjoy life more.'

Vision

'What will I be doing in ten years' time? What will I have accomplished?'

Think about yourself ten years from now. What picture comes to mind? How do you live your life? What are you proud of having achieved or accomplished? This is a very important part of your Brand Me Code. The very image you get when you ask yourself this question is valuable. You are able to see yourself in the future, the clearer the better. A lot of people live a whole life without any vision at all. The only good thing with this is that you never get disillusioned, but the bad thing is that you don't have any visual direction.

An example: 'My vision is to be known as a leading consultant within personal development for businesspeople within Europe and to have a small kennel for breeding spaniels, just for fun.'

Another example: 'Ten years from now I will be a respected authority within wireless e-learning applications, and I will have restored an old house by the lake I used to swim in as a child.'

Values

'What are my life rules, and what makes me trustworthy as a friend?'

The values are your rules of life, your deeper personality, elements that will make you valued as a friend and as trustworthy as a good brand. You need to be careful here. Try to find out what the real values are; check and double check.

An example: 'My values are freedom, integrity and simplicity.'

My Motto

Your Motto captures what you really stand for. It should be able to inspire you and guide you in almost any situation. It should help you to make decisions. It should help you to tell your story and create attention for you.

But the most important thing is that it should serve you as a personal mantra, rather than being something to communicate independently and directly.

If you like, you can use a well-known tag and either alter it to suit you, or role model on it and create something new but in the same style.

An example: 'Enjoy and Experience'.

Another example: 'Connecting Businesses'.

The Brand Me Code The Essence of What I Stand For

BENEFIT

What makes me useful to others?

POSITIONING

What makes me different, and/or more competent and/or more talented than others?

STYLE

What characterizes my style, my image, behaviour, tonality, etc.?

My Motto
Words or phrase, describing the essence of what I stand for

MISSION

What is my role in society, my issue, my larger responsibility or my passion in life?

VISION

What will I be doing in ten years' time? What will I have accomplished?

VALUES

What are my life rules, and what makes me trustworthy as a friend?

Creating my Brand Me Code

This is definitely something you must do with your honest self. The Brand Me Code is the essence of what you stand for. And it's what you want to stand for, not necessarily what other people think you stand for right now. There has to be room for improvement.

Start with the six inputs, and then create your motto.

STEP ONE – BENEFIT

Close your eyes, take a deep breath or two, and see yourself with your family, with your partner, your friends or at work. What you

feel comfortable doing is probably what you are good at. Open your eyes and make a list. Then make a choice of one or two benefits, and put them into a sentence.

Your Brand Me Mind Space will give you a lot of guidance. The Functional Dimension is important but other dimensions, like Social and Mental Dimensions, are also important here. Remember also what your friends appreciated about you, when you asked them about your Mind Space.

STEP TWO – POSITIONING

How do you differentiate yourself? From your list of benefits, select two or three of importance, combine these, and see what you get in the crossing of the two. It may result in an unusual combination. The more conflicting the benefits are in kind, the better.

The difference you make to others doesn't have to be that significant. Remember that a small difference can always be dramatized when communicated. For instance you may speak a very unusual foreign language, which may turn out to be a key factor when applying for a job. But, more importantly, it will make you feel different, and that is usually subconsciously communicated.

STEP THREE – STYLE

Close your eyes, take a deep breath or two, and see yourself coming towards you. How do you look? How do you walk? What are you wearing? Shake hands with yourself. How is your handshake? Is it firm? How do you present yourself? How is your voice, your tone? Does it feel good to meet yourself? What impression are you giving? Are you pleased with yourself?

If the image you see is the one you want to have, then write down a few key words describing and confirming your style. If you are not satisfied with something you saw, this is a good moment to re-program yourself. If there is something you really don't like in yourself, change it by visualizing that particular aspect of one of your role models. Then step back into the picture and copy them, doing it in just the same way. You can read more about this later in the book.

STEP FOUR – MISSION

Again, close your eyes, take a deep breath or two, and see yourself, but this time you are going onstage to receive an award. You feel the heat of the strong lights, the TV cameras make you a little bit nervous, but you are proud to be there anyway. What are you getting an award for? Listen carefully to the presenter and you'll now hear the reason. You feel great satisfaction; it's just as you expected, because you're being given the award for the very thing that you feel good about having contributed to, the thing that you feel responsible for and passionate about. What is that thing? What could it possibly be? Don't be afraid to scale up whatever interest or passion you have to a higher level, and put it into a bigger and more important context for society.

STEP FIVE – VISION

Daydream a little, take a deep breath and relax, close your eyes and take yourself on a trip into the future. See yourself in 10–15 years from now. What do you do for a living? What do you enjoy most? Do you have a family, or, if you have one already, what are they all doing? How about your present partner, your friends and colleagues? Try to meet them, look them in the face, ask them to smile and hear their voices when you ask them things. You can ask them whatever you like, for instance all the questions you ask yourself. What are you doing? Why have you become so successful? What have you accomplished? How did you get there?

STEP SIX – VALUES

In this step, we are in search of your own life rules, your principles in life.

A good way of finding your values and isolating them is to think about important areas in your life. For each of these areas you should identify what you feel is most important. It doesn't have to be just one thing: it can be several. If the same concept appears in more than one area, that's good.

The question to ask yourself is, what's so important about this area?

For example take the area of sport: what's so important about sport? The answer might be: 'challenge' or 'excitement'. Take the first word or words that come to mind!

The areas could be:

- family
- work
- travel
- friends
- health
- leisure
- sport
- relationships, and so on.

If you still find it difficult to express what's important, think about conflicts you may have had in a specific area. What was the fundamental value that you didn't want to compromise over?

Now, jot down the words that occur to you and circle those that appear in more than one area; also look for synonyms. If there are one or two more words that you feel are important enough, just add them to the list. Finally check the words by the value they would have in making you trustworthy to your best friend. Are there some other words that now come to mind? Can these words qualify as your life rules? Be choosy! Better a few strong important ones than a long list.

Here are some examples of personal values:

Aspiration
Autonomy
Beauty
Caring
Courage
Developing
Elegance
Fairness
Fun
Helping
Honesty
Humour
Individuality
Innovation
Inspirational
Joy
Justice
Learning
Love
Making revolutionary changes
Order
Perfection
Perseverance
Playfulness
Safety
Security
Simplicity
Synergy
Truth
Using abilities
Vitality
Wisdom
Wittiness

STEP SEVEN – CREATING MY MOTTO

Look at the result of all the six steps above in one glance; from them you will extract Your Motto. It doesn't have to be fantastic copy, as long as it means something to you. The point is you should later be able to make a story out of it that's both funny and interesting. Think about it for a while; be creative!

Now, check the quality of your Brand Me Code and your Motto. Does it give you strength in a possible conflict? Does it help you to choose between two job alternatives? Does it give guidance in relationships?

Take your time to evaluate if your Motto is the right one for you, if it captures what you want to stand for. To think of your Motto should be enough to give you direction and support in difficult situations!

CASE STUDY Driven by a mission

Geir, the quality software visionary

Geir was a physicist and computers were just tools for his research. But since they had to be programmed by the scientists themselves, Geir became a specialist in programming a certain processor.

A computer company also used this processor in air traffic control systems, and Geir was asked to come and work with them on this. First he declined, thinking it was below his level as a physicist ('Anyone could do this', he thought). But he changed his mind when offered a salary several times higher than he was earning as a scientist.

When he began to work with these critical software systems he was shocked at how low the quality of programming generally was. Later it also disturbed him that he had to sell systems to customers promising a quality that was not delivered.

This triggered Geir into starting a business of his own in quality software, which became his Mission, using all kinds of methods and process tools to help customers produce better software.

He began as a small entrepreneur but decided to get bigger with the help of venture capital and to aim for world-class customers, some of the very leading brands in the industrial world such as BMW, Volkswagen, Ericsson, ABB, Boeing, etc. He made this Vision of his very clear and inspired partners and employees to share it. He was able to imagine himself making business deals with some of the biggest companies in the world and having their logos in his presentations. This focus led to just that achievement: within four years Geir had managed to get all those world-class customers, which once seemed like a totally unrealistic dream. His company became world famous in the niche of quality software, which is now a growing area. In a society totally dependent on software with zero defects, the company is now well on its way to becoming a mainstream business.

Geir made his real breakthrough in the midst of the depression, when the rest of the IT industry was severely shaken. His company positioned itself very well in the complex software development market.

Geir is no doubt a strong personal brand and he has become just that by being very passionate, totally transparent as a personality and very focused. Above all he has demonstrated how important it is to have a vision.

03

chapter three

installing Brand Me – how to make the change

If you have followed the path of the book so far, you know what you stand for; you have your Motto, the underlying Benefit, Positioning, Style, Mission, Vision and Values. Now you are ready to do it! You are ready to put everything into your life. There are a few things that you have to consider when doing this.

Personal timeline – an important tool for change

Your life is a continuum of experiences. The personal timeline is a fundamental way to organize the personal events that have formed your life so far and will form your life in the future. Our attitudes to life are coded on the timeline and always connected to certain experiences. Our attitudes persist while we continue to get new experiences.

The Brand Me process and the Brand Me Code are definite milestones on your personal pathway or timeline. They will change your attitudes or strengthen them and will help you to look at your future experiences in a new way.

The personal timeline is one of the most important tools for change that you have access to and you should use it as much as you can, not only to go back in time but, more importantly, to look ahead.

This chapter is about how to install the Brand Me Code on your personal timeline, and re-program your settings for the future.

Let's start with making absolutely sure how *your* timeline looks and feels.

Changing your future – and your past

The thought of going back and changing history may sound crazy – this is something you are told you cannot do. But that is not true. With the personal timeline and the NLP techniques it's possible. And it is in fact necessary, since your life is largely run by your history, and the way that history has been allowed to interpret and form your opinions and personality. It hasn't asked for permission or for you to consciously decide what *you* want to stand for.

Your mind has been set on automatic pilot for so long. Now it's time to re-set it the way you want!

The fact is that you will now be able to go back on your timeline and clear up things in the past: negative programming, fear, mental obstacles, etc. There are two reasons for doing this. Firstly, it's a way of getting rid of things in your past that don't work for you, memories that give you bad feelings even today and disturb your life.

But the more important reason for going back and cleaning up is to erase or re-program patterns that will decide how you will experience things in the future. If, for instance, you have a fear of speaking in public because of an event earlier on your timeline, this may stop you from being able to be perceived as your desired Brand Me, because you will never be able to speak for yourself in public.

Discover your personal timeline

This little exercise will help you to identify your own timeline. You will need this to be able to do the 'Brand Me Installer' later.

STEP ONE

Find a good comfortable position and take a minute to relax. Take a second to clear your mind by thinking about something mundane, for example brushing your teeth or something else you do regularly.

STEP TWO

Now when you have this mundane activity in mind, think about an occasion when you did it a month ago, and then a specific occasion six months ago, a year ago, five years ago and then ten years ago. Think of all these occasions at the same time. Notice how they now arrange themselves in your mind. For many of us, images in the mind form a line, arranging themselves with the latest memory closest and the most distant memories furthest away. Notice how you see your line: is it straight or curved? Is it behind you or beside you? It doesn't matter how you see it, any way is fine; it's the way your brain has found it practical to organize it.

STEP THREE

Let's look into the future. Where do you see it? Again, you take the same ordinary event or another that you would expect to happen regularly and put the recurrences into your future: a week from now, a month, a year, five years, ten years, etc. Think of all these occasions at once again and see how they arrange themselves to form your future timeline. See which direction your images are taking. The directions are different for most of us: it could be to the left, the right or straight in front of us.

STEP FOUR

The whole of your timeline is now forming. How does it look taken together? Is it straight, is it curved, is it v-shaped? Establish where you are at the present. Does the timeline pass through you, or are you standing in the bottom of a 'v'? It doesn't matter how it appears to you. The most important thing is that you have now discovered and become familiar with your personal timeline.

Disruption is the key to change

Disrupting your patterns and re-programming yourself is basically what it's all about. There are some great benefits to be reaped from achieving a state of disruption. This is actually what's happening when you go into 'altered states of mind', in other words, daydreaming, meditation, self-hypnosis, etc.

An example of how our mind works is the 'Handshake Interruption' that Richard Bandler, one of the founders of NLP, uses as a method of quickly introducing an altered state of mind, allowing him to access and then re-program someone's behaviour.

It works like this: you attempt to shake someone's hand, and it's so automatic that if you put out your hand most people will take and shake it. Now you disrupt this automatic pattern by changing the direction of your hand and *not* grasping the other person's. What happens then is a moment of confusion: a pattern is broken. A therapist can use this in order to get access to a person's mind.

Now you have to make this disruption on your own. Begin with mapping what big patterns you have, running your life for you. Look at all aspects of your life. Why not begin with your relationships? What relationships are most important to you? And why? Try to figure out if they are balanced. Don't forget relationships with your parents or sisters and brothers, even if you don't meet them that often. Then move on to work relationships, including other commitments like societies or activities that you are involved in.

Most of these patterns you should maintain, because they're convenient and they work well, or fairly well. But maybe there is one pattern in particular that you find both important and irritating, a pattern you really want to change.

The Brand Me Installer

This is a technique that you can use to 'install' your Brand Me on your timeline, and thus be able to change existing patterns and key situations in your past over and over again, as well as program your future.

STEP ONE

Find a relaxing place. Close your eyes if you want. Make yourself comfortable. Begin by looking off to your right. Imagine seeing someone who looks just like you a short distance away. This 'other you' will do all the learning in this exercise; you are only observing.

STEP TWO

This other you *is* your Brand Me, applying your Brand Me Code, your Motto, acting out your new Brand Me to perfection. See this other you in detail: clothes, gestures, image, behaviour, etc. Hear the voice. Feel this other you! Take some time to do this. Be impressed by that other you, performing your Brand Me so well!

STEP THREE

Think of a situation in your life that has influenced your attitudes and your behaviour in a negative way, when you really could have done with having your strong and positive Brand Me. Take your time to find one such occasion, then you can go back and find another, and so on. See the situation as it unfolded before; look at it from a distance as if it were a movie. Watch the actors, including yourself, and what they do. Rewind the 'tape' of the situation, and go to the moment *just before* it becomes bad; pause!

STEP FOUR

Now let your Brand Me step in and take over the action at that very point just before it gets bad. Watch the Brand Me perform your previous part in the way you would expect from your Brand Me.
Be satisfied with the scene only when you feel really good about the result of your Brand Me acting out yourself in this situation. Keep changing and adjusting the acting as if you were the director until you are totally satisfied. How does the picture change? Does it become brighter, more colourful, larger and three-dimensional? How does it sound? What feeling do you get from seeing it? If it isn't as bright, colourful, etc. as you want, or the sound is not as 'live' as you want, make it so! If you don't feel as good as you want, do it again until you are completely satisfied!

STEP FIVE

When you are fully satisfied with the Brand Me action in the situation, integrate the 'other you', who *is* your Brand Me, completely into yourself. You can reach out your arms and imagine drawing the Brand Me into yourself. You may experience a feeling of tingle or a release of energy when doing this. You have now 'installed' the Brand Me in you.

STEP SIX

You are now ready to travel your personal timeline. Keep in mind your positive feeling about your newly installed Brand Me. Imagine floating out of your body above your timeline, which you have discovered in the previous exercise. Go back in time as far as you ▶

want (you can do this exercise over and over again and go further back each time). Continue to move rapidly forward through all your past memories towards your present. Experience how these past memories are also instantly changed and enriched by your Brand Me, in the same way as the situation that you used to first install the Brand Me was changed. Stop at the present. Now feel how the Brand Me will help you to transform future experiences as well. You feel great about the future and confident in your Brand Me.

You can do this exercise several times in order to strengthen the benefits from it.

Taking action and becoming true to your Brand Me

From your decision to apply your Brand Me will flow various consequential decisions. Some of these are very simple; it may be things like a new wardrobe, or to learn certain skills, etc. But some decisions will involve much larger undertakings.

It's not unusual for people who do the Brand Me program to change a lot of things in their lives, though of course in a positive way. During the process so far you may already have seen exactly what you need to change. Or you may not be able to grasp it in detail yet. It doesn't matter if you have or have not.

The only thing that matters is that you feel in charge of your life.

A good idea is to go through this little checklist:

- Am I living my Motto?
- Am I living out my Mission?
- Am I directing my life towards my Vision?
- Am I being true to my Values?

- Am I acting according to my Style?
- Am I living up to my Positioning and my competence?
- Am I influencing my environment the way I want?

Enhance your charisma – get aligned

It's sometimes called charisma, enthusiasm, excitement, zest or passion. It goes under many names because it's so extremely important for personal success. Congruence is what it's called in NLP terminology. Congruence means that all of you, all parts of you, are aligned with what you are doing at the moment.

You have probably experienced it many times: everything seems to be in sync, your voice is strong and persuasive, you feel the power.

But you may also have experienced the opposite: you have tried your best in a meeting, but instead of focusing on the relevant issues your mind has wandered to other things, paying the monthly bills or having jealous thoughts about what your partner is doing on a business trip. You will have noticed how your performance and maybe the whole meeting are affected by your lack of congruence.

The interesting thing with incongruence is that we may be able to focus on our verbal communication, but what gives us away is the non-verbal, like glancing out of the window, looking at our watch, making nervous body movements, tapping with our foot, etc. This soon becomes the most important communication in your meeting; it doesn't matter that you are able to handle the verbal communication in a disciplined way when the non-verbal is so undisciplined. Studies show that 80% of our communication is non-verbal.

Incongruence is usually something that you actually feel physically. Below you'll find an exercise that you can do to localize and feel the signs of both congruence and incongruence.

You might be totally motivated to live your Brand Me, but an inner feeling that is out of sync with the rest of you may thwart all your good intentions.

We tend to have a lot of fears that stop us from taking the action we have decided upon. It could be a variety of feelings stopping us, like intimidation, jealousy, self-righteousness or general insecurity about our ability.

Your usual strategy may be just to override those feelings. But to escape from feelings like that by shoving them under the carpet never works. We all know that from experience ... yet we keep on doing it!

It's like when you are holding a balloon down under water: as soon as you let go and don't consciously keep holding it down, up it pops!

The way you have to deal with all the obstacles in the way of becoming aligned and congruent is to negotiate. Never try to escape!

The Charisma Controller

This is a tool for you to use to detect when you are incongruent. You may find it useful because incongruence can be difficult to be aware of if you are not trained to listen to the signals. Of course it also gets you acquainted with the feeling of total alignment, and to be able to re-create that is very motivating when you are living your Brand Me.

STEP ONE

Try to think of a situation where you know you have experienced incongruence. Now try to go back and remember the details, and how you felt.

STEP TWO

Try to re-create the feeling, and try to figure out which parts of your body signalled to you that they were not taking part, sharing or getting involved. In such situations it's very common for people to feel that 'something is wrong' in the chest or stomach area. Where exactly do you feel it, and how does it feel? Fix that feeling in your memory. Now try to call it up again! Then relax a little.

STEP THREE

Now think of a time when you experienced total congruence and re-create that in your mind. What do you see? What do you hear? What do you feel? Try to locate the bodily signs of the total alignment, the total congruence. Typically you'll have an unusual sensation. It may be difficult to put into words; it may be something you just intuitively know! People sometimes say they feel a lightness, an openness, a being drawn forward, usually in the chest. Find a word or sound for that feeling; say the word or the sound when you feel that feeling.

STEP FOUR

Finally compare the different feelings of incongruence and congruence. Be particularly aware of where in the body the feelings are located. Switch from one feeling to the other.

STEP FIVE

By doing this and becoming familiar with the signs of when you are aligned with yourself and when not, you will improve your performance a lot. When you are feeling incongruence in a situation when you need to be aligned, think about the part of the body where you have the feeling of congruence, and your congruence pattern will be switched on.

Negotiate Brand Me with yourself

This is the time, but not before now, to look for obstacles and ask some very important questions about the consequences of the Brand Me that you have decided to go for.

There are always critical questions: some of them will immediately reinforce your support for your Brand Me, some will put the whole thing in question and make it feel impossible ever to apply it.

All objections contain important information about how you can carry out the task of applying Brand Me. You just have to listen to these inner objections and respect them.

Here are some of the key questions:

- How does my Brand Me relate to my job and my responsibilities at work?
- How does my Brand Me relate to my relationships: my partner, my family and my friends?
- How does my Brand Me relate to all my other activities?
- How does my Brand Me relate to my community and my near future?

Set aside plenty of time to think about these questions and listen carefully to any part of you that objects to your Brand Me Code. It's very important for success with your personal branding to handle any objections with respect. When an objection arises, you have to respond. How you deal with these objections is crucial for the alignment inside yourself and for creating congruence.

You have to negotiate with all these objections, and the parts of you that hold these objections, just as if they were people you really cared about. Sometimes the objections may also concern the implications for other people and you have to make a negotiation 'out there'. But more important is what goes on 'inside' you.

Beware of trying to convince yourself about doing something by just squashing an inner objection.

This could result in a lack of self-confidence in applying the rest of the Brand Me.

Here are the steps:

- Listen to your inner objections.
- Look for a positive intention and deeper value behind them.
- Create new and different ways to achieve these values!
- Negotiate a deal that makes it work for all of you.

Let's take an example of the sort of objections that can arise. Your inner voice tells you that your partner in life will not accept your Brand Me, since it may change your life quite dramatically (you may have a desire to do voluntary work in Africa). What is the positive value that lies behind your concern?

Probably you care for your partner, and maybe this will lead to a discussion with them and a possible arrangement that allows them to be involved in the change in one way or another. Your negotiation with yourself might alternatively lead to the conclusion that this objection should be handled by splitting from your partner, since you don't share the same values or mission.

Another objection might be that what you want to do is very dangerous. The positive thing with this is that you will then know how happy you are to be alive, and you will feel responsible for your partner and the family. This is a good value. How it can be turned into something positive, maybe the choice of a safer way to do this, is what the negotiation aims to determine.

CASE STUDY Be honest with yourself

Sophie

In her twenties Sophie worked as a marketing assistant. During the first years everything was great. She was developing herself and getting more and more responsibility; in the beginning she felt the responsibility was perhaps too much, but she grew into the role. She was going abroad frequently to visit associates and subsidiaries in Europe and to attend marketing conferences. 'Really good fun,' she thought and got absorbed by her career. But after a few years a strange feeling started to creep up on her and she began to ask herself 'What do I really know?', 'What do I create?' Lots of questions concerning her skills and inner core attacked her. But she couldn't talk about that with many people: they all said that she had this fantastic glamorous job!

After a period of confusion, she was then 26 or 27 years old – she came across copywriting. It felt very satisfying: she felt that she was creating something, also something that came from within. It took away the emptiness she had started to feel at work.

She reflected much on her future. Her heart said that she should quit her job and apply for art school to study copywriting. Her rational mind objected, saying that she had deliberately chosen an international path and that she eventually wanted to live abroad. In addition being a copywriter would mean that she started from scratch again – first living as a student with no income, and then embarking on a new career. It would also mean that she would have to stay on the domestic job market for a few years to come. In that particular profession your best chances of working abroad come when you are more senior; then you can concentrate on ideas and concepts rather than doing the actual writing.

But there was only one way to go. She made her mind up when she was accepted at art school. Inner satisfaction must conquer.

Today, after a few years of hard work in her home country she is now working internationally again but this time on a more fulfilling level, combining her earlier corporate experiences with creative work.

04

chapter four

packaging Brand Me – now even better

This chapter is not about how to change your looks. Plastic surgery and cosmetics are not within our remit. No, it's entirely about how to make the most of your existing personality, by being aware of what you want to achieve and what you stand for on a deeper personal level.

Say you are shy. You don't need to be a performer. If you are not, you could use your shyness to your advantage and concentrate on communicating a more profound personality. The quiet personality can easily become an interesting one; you just have to be aware that this is your strategy and be more patient about results and feedback. A more open personality gets feedback faster, but this won't necessarily be a winning strategy in the long run if it's not your natural style.

There is a talent in every one of us for packaging.

You have to find a style that matches your personality rather than trying to do something totally contrasting, looking for a quick effect by changing personality.

The Brand Me Story – presentation of yourself

Up to this point we have focused on the first major step in creating a brand – **differentiation**, being different. That's what we have done by creating the Brand Me Code. Now it's time for the next major step – to **dramatize**.

Madonna

Madonna definitely belongs to the elite of personal branding. She is probably the strongest female brand in the history of modern entertainment.

What is Madonna's recipe? Hard work for sure, but more than anything else it's conscious styling. It started very much as 'girl power' – 'I'll make it on my own' – and it continued as the attitude of the more mature independent female.

Madonna has mastered the knack of picking up trends early, integrating them into herself, interpreting them in her own way and launching them with dramatic effect and perfect timing. She has a feel for when the market is ready.

Madonna Brand Me Mind Space

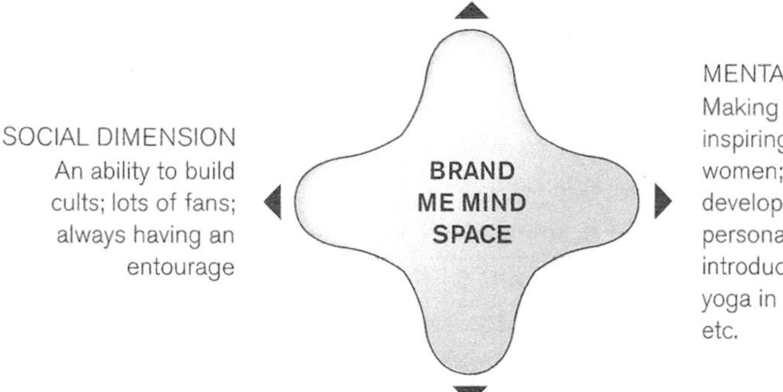
FUNCTIONAL DIMENSION
Design and packaging of performance, styling and trendy music
SOCIAL DIMENSION
An ability to build cults; lots of fans; always having an entourage
BRAND ME MIND SPACE
MENTAL DIMENSION
Making it on your own, inspiring a lot of women; an ability to develop her personality, introducing meditation, yoga in her own way, etc.
SPIRITUAL DIMENSION
Involved in charity concerts, however not taken any issue of her own (yet) – a potential here to further stretch her personal branding!

Packaging a personality is all about dramatization; it's acting out the character described in the script. To sell yourself successfully you have to truly act out what is you, or rather, what you have just decided that you *want* to be.

To be an actor on stage, first of all you have to have a script. The basis for this is the Brand Me Code, but you also have to write dialogue (or maybe rather monologue), you have to choose or design your costume, to direct your expression, your voice, your gestures and your general way of moving around.

Let's start with how to create a good story out of you, a good script.

First you have to fill the story structure with content, in other words back to the differentiation.

In order to do this in a very easy way, take your Brand Me Code (with Benefit, Position, Style, Mission, Vision, Values and Your Motto) and the 4-D Brand Me Mind Space (Functional, Social, Mental and Spiritual Dimensions).

Structure the dramatization

There are many ways to describe the basic rules of dramatization. One of the best at this is Syd Field, creator of the bible of screenwriting *The Screenwriter's Workbook,* without which no screenwriter in Hollywood could ever function. The fact is that most Hollywood productions are based on the structure he describes. What could be better than using a screenwriter's structure when building your Brand Me Story?

Syd Field claims that the first step in the screenwriting process is the subject. In screenwriting this means you identify first the main character, then the action, and then you are able in a few words to describe the subject of the film. The good news in our case is that we already have the character – YOU, and the action – everything that's in your Brand Me Code.

The structure of screenwriting consists of three steps, or acts. They are the basic steps in all stories, folktales included. That's why the structure proves very helpful in creating the dramatic structure of the Brand Me Story too. The three acts are:

Act 1. Beginning	Set-up	Presentation: who you are, your relationships
Act 2. Middle	Confrontation	The problem; obstacles and conflicts
Act 3. End	Resolution	How the problem is solved

Act 1 sets up the story and must therefore be crafted carefully. It has to catch the attention of the audience. It's the typical one-liner; who am I, what do I do, how can I interest you?

At the end of the first act the screenwriter (or storyteller) introduces something interesting, or exciting, that drives us into Act 2. Syd Field calls this Plot Point 1 (in our example below it's the mention of 'personal branding').

Act 2 builds up the problem, the obstacle and the conflict. In our Brand Me Story it has to quickly address a problem that the audience can identify with (in the example below, 'the fast pace of change').

At the end of Act 2, Plot Point 2 appears, again a point when you introduce something that can drive forward the interest, or excitement, this time into Act 3. It also points at a solution, which can be further explained in Act 3.

Act 3 gives and explains the solutions to the problem. It also ties in with Act 1, enabling us to come full circle: we end where we started but in an enlightened way and on a higher level. We have communicated something of interest, and have created a situation of 'wanting to know more' and maybe the beginning of a new relationship, business or personal.

An example

The Brand Me Story (monologue) of Anette Rosencreutz:

'I'm a communications and branding consultant who specializes in *personal branding* (Plot Point 1) [helping companies and people to find out what they stand for] (Functional Dimension; Set-up). I have worked with some of the leading companies in Scandinavia, for example Ericsson (Social Dimension; Set-up). In today's fast-paced and constantly changing world (Confrontation) it's crucial to quickly make the right decisions; therefore you must know what you stand for, both as a person and a company. I have a *special four-dimensional method* (Plot Point 2) for doing that (Mental Dimension); it's basically about improving communication both in business and in your private life (Spiritual Dimension; Resolution).'

We have put 'helping companies and people to find out what they stand for' in square brackets because you could take this out and still have a good Brand Me Story, but sometimes it's nice to be a little more specific. In this case it's the phrase: 'you must know what you stand for' that really makes the story.

Put the story in a dialogue mode

In real life you would usually have a dialogue inviting you to improvise on your script and story. You will find out how easily you can use the questions you are asked to promote your story, just as media-trained people, like top executives and politicians, are supposed to do. You can also learn how to use your answers to set the agenda for the next question.

A good way to practise how to take your story into a dialogue is to set yourself in a debate situation. The simple technique is to think up all the possible objections to your story; be very nasty and suspicious and critical. Put the objecting questions on paper. Now go about answering them, using your basic story but with explanations and elaborations, of course.

Here is Anette's story again, cast in a dialogue form:

Q. What do you do?

A. I'm a communications and branding consultant who specializes in personal branding. (Functional Dimension)

Q. What do you mean by that?

A. I help people and companies to find out what they stand for. (Functional/Mental Dimension)

Q. Who are your clients?

A. It's both people and companies; I work for some of the leading Scandinavian companies, such as Ericsson. But I also work in the UK and in the US. (Social Dimension)

Q. How does a company benefit from personal branding?

A. A company with individuals who know what they stand for performs better, has more drive, better leaders and better teamwork, and earns greater respect from others. We also do teamwork sessions based on personal branding. (Mental/Social Dimension)

Q. What happens if a person finds out that he or she stands for something completely different from what their company stands for and as a result leaves the company?

A. It's better for both to find out about a mismatch at an early stage: it saves a lot of frustration and inefficiency. (Spiritual Dimension)

The Brand Me performance – your action on stage

Performance is about role modelling. All your life you have been role modelling on others: your parents, your brother or sister, your friends, your teachers, your colleagues or bosses at work. You've seldom had a conscious choice of role models; it was made by your subconscious mind. But now you'll have a conscious choice.

We have met people who find it strange that we recommend the use of role models when you are supposed to become a brand yourself – differentiated from others. It's an interesting objection. But the truth is that everything you model is already a part of yourself. You will never be able to copy someone exactly anyhow: it will be your version integrated into yourself and therefore unique.

All actors have this problem when they have to play a role. They have all had role models in order to find their own expression, voice and presentation. Usually an actor has a mix of role models: these can be other actors, but they can also be people that they have come across in their private life.

Paradoxically, to access your own behaviour you will have to go through someone else, and establish the way you would like to perform. That's the only way you will be able to do yourself justice!

Remember that the script you are playing, you have created yourself and feel passionate about. You are also your own director, giving yourself direction! Being the scriptwriter and director at the same time as the actor ensures that it's you who performs and no one else.

What happens is that you get this subconsciously into your mind, so that you'll never have to think about it. It will be like riding a bicycle: you don't think about doing it once it's programmed into your subconscious mind!

Pick up your performance

This is the quick guide to an improved performance in addition to the 'style' you have already decided for your Brand Me Code. It's fast, but efficient. The idea is to re-program yourself so that your appearance is aligned with your Brand Me Code.

During this entire exercise you should imagine that everything is happening as if in a movie. Imagine yourself sitting in the darkness of a movie theatre and watch!

STEP ONE

Close your eyes; see yourself as in a movie, coming towards you to greet you.

How do you look? Pay attention to detail. What do you wear? What impression do you give? What do you signal? What do you seem to represent: business, organization, values, background, social position?

How do you sound? Listen to your voice telling your Brand Me Story. How does it sound? Convincing? Do you speak with passion?

How do you appear? How do you move? How does your handshake feel (is it energetic, does it give off a feeling of security or does it suggest that you are under stress and insecure)?

Are you satisfied with yourself? Are you aligned with your Brand Me Code?

If not, what do you want to change?

STEP TWO

Find a person to role model on. Maybe you have one in mind already, someone you really admire for being good at communicating themselves.

Pay special attention to the people who irritate you by being so much better and more successful than you: envy is a very good driver to use when searching for a role model. Maybe you have told yourself when you watch this person that it's just an act and that you could probably do it yourself if you wanted to. Now here is the opportunity: do it – copy that person, in detail!

How does he/she speak: tone of voice, words, clarity, pace, expressions, language, etc.?

How does he/she appear: gestures, general behaviour, handshake, pace, manners, postures, eye movements, etc.?

How does he/she look: style of clothes, shoes, grooming, accessories? Is it in sync with what he/she represents (kind of business, type of organization, background, social position, etc.)? If not, what effect does the contrast have (is it positive, questionable or negative)? How does the person order his or her environment?

Notice all these things and make sense of them, a sense that works for you!

If at all possible, let the role model correct you. Sometimes, of course, this is difficult to do, for example if you are modelling someone covertly.

STEP THREE

Now put this person, the role model, into your situation on the movie screen, playing your part, presenting your Brand Me Code and doing your story, carrying out your role at work, for example. The more detail you put into this, the better.

STEP FOUR

Finally, see yourself taking over the role of your role model: copy the behaviour exactly; try to really get into the act.

This time you don't see yourself acting: you are actually on the screen *yourself* and performing.

You are filled with your role, doing your story, you hear your voice, you feel the live feeling, and you see the people you meet and how they respond with interest and admiration. And you really feel how well you are being yourself, how perfectly you perform! You know beforehand this will be a great success!

Princess Diana

A modern British royal, one of the strongest international personal brands not only in the royal community, but also in society as a whole, Princess Diana had already become an icon even before her tragic death.

She became a role model for many women because of her openness in the media about her feelings and sensibility. She combined her busy public life with being a caring mother, raising her children with love and also preparing them for life by consciously introducing them to its realities.

Princess Diana Brand Me Mind Space

FUNCTIONAL DIMENSION
A modern British royal and ambassador for Britain, combining public life with being a loving mother, preparing her children for the realities of life

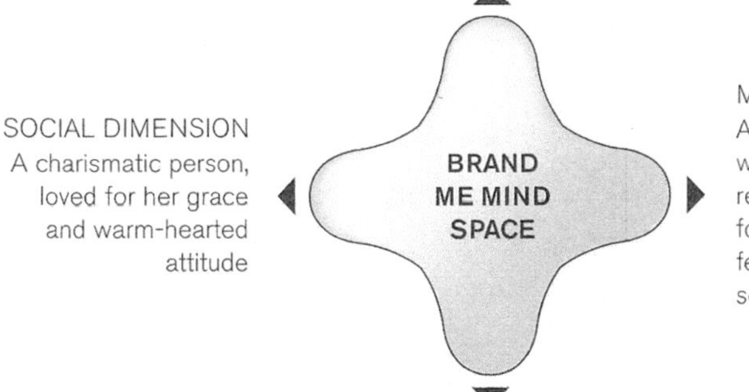

BRAND
ME MIND
SPACE
SOCIAL DIMENSION
A charismatic person, loved for her grace and warm-hearted attitude

MENTAL DIMENSION
A role model for women both with regard to style and for daring to show her feelings and sensibility

SPIRITUAL DIMENSION
Much engaged in charity, also in controversial issues like Aids and land mines, the latter being her main issue in her last years

part three
launching Brand Me

05

chapter five

activating Brand Me – setting the agenda

Look at your Brand Me Mind Space and compare it with what you are today; maybe you'll have some gaps to fill in. This is the 'product development' or 'R&D' that a company would set out to do in the same situation.

Of course this development should be led by your Brand Me Code; here you'll find the indications of what needs to be done.

For most people this is about education and training in different skills. But it may also include a lot of communication, using symbols and rituals to create your own myth. You might also need to quickly re-program yourself in certain specific situations that might stop you from being what you want to be in the minds of other people. An example of such a situation might be public speaking. In this chapter we will deal with all this and more.

Creating your own myth

If you role model on the most successful personal brand builders, you will notice they all have one thing in common: there are a lot of good stories about them. These stories are filled with symbols and rituals that these people enact to create a place in people's minds.

Rituals like these have to come from within: authenticity is crucial. You have to generate your symbols and rituals from your Brand Me Code: it's a way to dramatize the difference encapsulated in that code of yours.

The myths of IKEA founder Ingvar Kamprad

A good example of myths that drive the brand of a whole worldwide organization are the stories told about Ingvar Kamprad; some of them are probably true, but some are apocryphal, of course. It doesn't matter; they are great pieces of personal marketing as well as an excellent way of communicating company values.

STEP ONE

When he visits any of his worldwide stores he performs certain rituals. For example he might pick up a piece of furniture thrown into the garbage (maybe by himself just beforehand) and tell the staff that he doesn't want to see such waste: the 'damaged' goods could be sold off cheaply instead.

STEP TWO

He asks customers at the counter about their perception of the value of a product they have just bought. 'Is it really worth its price?' is an example of the sort of question he might ask. He persists until the customer says 'No' or repeats their 'Yes' frequently enough for him to be satisfied. Then he knows if the price is right or not.

STEP THREE

One of many stories about his extreme cost-consciousness. When inaugurating a statue of himself in his hometown Älmhult, he wouldn't cut the ribbon, but instead untied it and gave it back to the mayor, saying 'You can use it again.'

It's much better to be spontaneous when exploring possible activities. The chance that you will actually follow through is much greater when the ideas are generated with intuition.

The best way to generate ideas on how to communicate is to use your Brand Me Code and your Motto as a starting point and work the ideas out in the four dimensions of your Brand Me Mind Space in order to stretch the Mind Space the way you expect it to be stretched in the minds of other people.

We are talking about all sorts of ideas, from what you need in order to develop yourself to the way you could create symbols and rituals representing what you want to stand for.

The Brand Me Activity Generator

The Brand Me Activity Generator is a simple but effective device that will prove useful to you in producing new ideas about how you can develop yourself and communicate yourself based on your Brand Me Code and your Motto. It organizes your thinking in the four dimensions, helping you to fill in the gaps between the Brand Me Mind Space you want to occupy in other people's minds and what you feel that you do today.

STEP ONE

Put your Motto in the centre of the Brand Me Activity Generator.

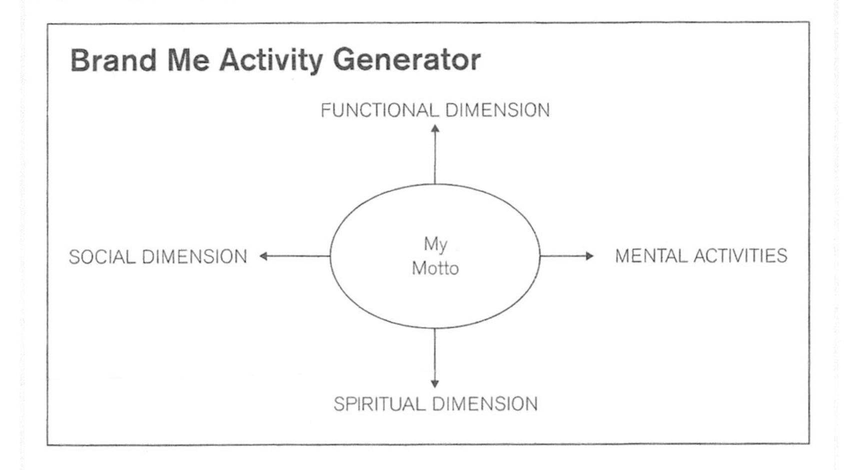

STEP TWO

Think about the different activities you might undertake to stretch the perception of yourself in the Mind Space of different stakeholders (you may later need to do a separate Brand Me Activity Generator for each particular stakeholder category) and to communicate what you stand for (your Brand Me Code/Motto).

Start with the Functional Dimension. For example, what training could you do to improve yourself functionally? Is there some knowledge that it would be useful to acquire? Use the entire Brand Me Code to get ideas.

STEP THREE

Then do the same for the Social Dimension. How can you fulfil your expected Brand Me Mind Space, using your Motto/Brand Me

Code for guidance? Activities here could include becoming a member of different social groups, clubs or associations. Or you could just think about social networking opportunities at work.

STEP FOUR

Same thing with the Mental Dimension. How could you develop yourself to become a mentor and adviser in your field with your Motto/Brand Me Code? This may be a long-term project, but it has to start some time – so why not now?

STEP FIVE

Finally your Spiritual Dimension. What do you need to be connected to the larger perspective in life, the way you have described it in your Brand Me Mind Space? Here you could also go to the Mission in your Brand Me Code for ideas. The answers you give may also be connected with your Social Dimension, taking part in some social activity with a higher local or global purpose, for example.

STEP SIX

The outcome of this workshop with yourself is a list of activities and ideas for how to develop yourself, a list that needs to be prioritized and scheduled. Some activities may be quickly done, whereas some may take a very long time to accomplish.

Speak for yourself

The skill most people consider to be the trickiest to master is public speaking. Yet at the same time this is also the very skill most want to improve upon in order to fulfil their expectations of themselves.

A good example of this is an elite Swedish woman golfer, one of the stars on the golf World Tour. She had this problem of always coming in second. Until the last few holes she was usually leading, and then she would make some totally inexplicable mistakes and just didn't seem to be able to keep up her good play to the end of the game and winning. Of course she tried a lot of things with her trainer, especially her mental trainer, a very insightful person who listened to her saying one day how much she hated to talk to the press after a game. The trainer immediately understood that this could be the whole reason for her never winning: subconsciously she didn't want to win because she would have to make a speech. Of course once this was explained to her she then took action and began training in public speaking.

Sir Sean Connery

Sir Sean Connery is one of the strongest living brands in the world of movies. Although his fame started with his portrayal of James Bond, he was able to leave this permanently behind and create an almost stronger personal brand.

Sir Sean Connery Brand Me Mind Space

FUNCTIONAL DIMENSION
A productive and extremely skilled actor with broad talents, playing characters that appear to be very much aligned with himself

SOCIAL DIMENSION
Has the largest and most dedicated fan club among older actors, seems to be a very sociable person in his private life especially on and around the golf course

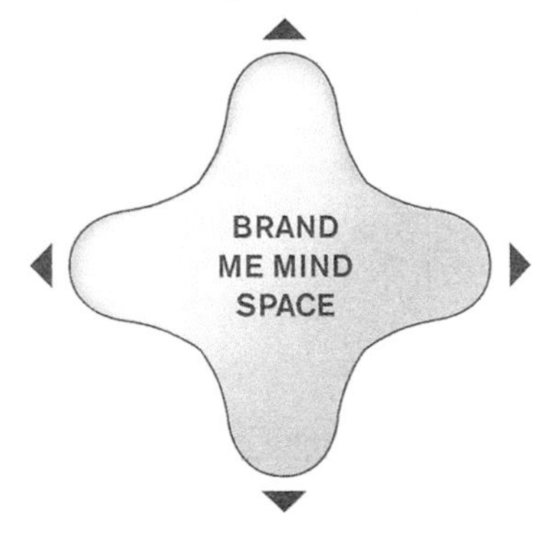

MENTAL DIMENSION
Role model for actors and for all (ageing) men: chosen as the world's sexiest man when in his sixties; a 'real man' with a deeper personality

SPIRITUAL DIMENSION
Genuine and strong interest in supporting the Scottish nation and young Scots from less fortunate backgrounds to get a good education

He did this by stretching his Mind Space in all four dimensions. Apart from being a good actor and having a strong Functional Dimension, Sean Connery has also become the Scottish Nationalist Movement's most dedicated and publicly known celebrity supporter, typically the only one to wear a kilt at the first opening of the Scottish Parliament.

The Brand Me Switch

You can actually use the Brand Me Installer, described in Chapter 3, to change a specific behaviour like a problem with appearing in public, which can be hard to change with conscious training only

STEP ONE

Go back to the situation on your Personal Timeline that you remember as the one that caused your problem, and right at the beginning of that sequence just before things get bad, you pause. Then you simply replace the less competent versions of yourself with your Brand Me.

STEP TWO

Take your time to do this, make the image brighter, more 'alive' and more convincing. Don't stop until you are really satisfied.

STEP THREE

The Brand Me can be used as switch, whenever you want to change from a bad behaviour that you feel you are stuck with into something new different, competent or attractive, that you really want to be like. And you can do it as many times as you like. It just makes you better!

06

chapter six

marketing Brand Me – time for action

In this chapter we will structure all the things that until now you have more or less intuitively experienced into a marketing plan for marketing your Brand Me. It's time to consciously think about what the outcome of this whole exercise should be, and how to get there.

We will work through three important questions. These are:

- **why** – targets and objectives
- **who** – audiences and stakeholders
- **how** – choosing communication channels.

The fourth question that is a part of any classic marketing strategy is one you have already answered: '**what** to communicate'. That is, of course, your Brand Me including your Motto, and developed into your Brand Me Story.

Finding the market where your change will make a difference

You may as a result of doing this process have come to some very difficult but important conclusions. Maybe there is no need in your environment or workplace for a person like the Brand Me you have decided upon.

The problem is that people tend to see you as you have always been.

You may have decided in your Brand Me exercise to be a serious, more intellectual person, for example, but your friends see you in the same way as you have been for years, as the happy clown, always funny but never really serious; they will never really accept your attempt to change.

Alternatively, let's say you are shy and have a tendency to feel awkward in public. You may now decide to train that part of your personality and the result is a much more confident and secure you. If you now introduce yourself to new acquaintances this is the way they will perceive you from the very start. Your old friends, however, will remember your more insecure personality for evermore.

Why – what are my objectives and targets?

Here you have to be really true to yourself. What is your most important reason for doing your Brand Me process? What do you really want? What is most important for you right *now*? Which of the following achievements would fill you with the most satisfaction?

- Changing job.
- Meeting a partner.
- Getting a larger social network.

- Becoming a leader.
- Taking the next step in life.
- Having a better relationship with your partner.
- Being taken more seriously.
- Developing skills.
- Being a good father or mother.
- Becoming a better public speaker.
- Getting some appreciation or becoming a star at work.
- Impressing your friends.

Or is there something else?

It's important that you think this through consciously. Go back to your Brand Me Code and Vision and Mission for inspiration.

Maybe you want to do many things? Then prioritize: work on one achievement at a time, if possible. If you can't avoid working on several at once, make each one a separate project on which to focus, check and report back to yourself.

Visualize your situation or situations in detail. Make them into a movie; see yourself going on stage and actually doing and becoming what you want …

If you find it difficult to come up with a clear target, move on to the next section and think about it from the point of view of your stakeholders. Which ones do you want to become more branded for?

Who is my audience, or my stakeholders?

The audience is the stakeholders in your life, everyone who has expectations of you. Each stakeholder wants different things from you, usually a mixture: things ranging from love, advice and support to your special professional skills. They all want time, devotion and attention.

These could very well be some of your stakeholders:

- life partner
- family: mother, father, brothers and sisters, children if you have any
- friends, of all kinds: friends from childhood, new friends, acquaintances
- colleagues
- clients
- employer, or business partners if you have your own business
- employees, if you are the boss, and so on.

When you do this little exercise you realize that you can't possibly please them all. And that is the reason why you need a strategy in order to make life manageable.

Now go back to your targets and prioritize your stakeholders!

Gérard Depardieu

The French super-actor famous abroad for, among other things, his portrayal of Cyrano de Bergerac, the large-nosed, unattractive, but charming swordsman and brilliant poet. Also internationally famous for his equally brilliant acting in *The Count of Monte Cristo* and numerous other films. Depardieu the man is also impressive, having a genuine, relaxed and charming manner.

His Functional Dimension is obvious from his acting abilities, his great mental alignment with his characters making them become extraordinarily alive and real.

His Social Dimension is demonstrated by his genuinely sociable character and charismatic personality. He is loved by many people, has a large fan club and is very French in his lifestyle, enjoying good food and wine.

His Mental Dimension produces a role model for many men: not being classically good looking and rather corpulent, he nevertheless has stature, charm, charisma, curiosity and interest in self-development. In one interview he commented on his acquisition of a vineyard and consequent need to learn about winemaking in the following terms: 'You have to be allowed to be a beginner in one area, even if you are experienced in another.'

Being a warm-hearted person he does a lot of charity work as his Spiritual Dimension. He's also often invited to represent French culture internationally, together with the president of France.

Gérard Depardieu Brand Me Mind Space

FUNCTIONAL DIMENSION
A talented and classically skilled actor

SOCIAL DIMENSION
A genuinely French sociable character and a charismatic personality; loved by many people; has a large fan club

MENTAL DIMENSION
A role model for many men: though not clasically good looking he has stature, charm, charisma and interest in self-development

SPIRITUAL DIMENSION
A warm-hearted and socially conscious person doing lots of charity work; represents French culture internationally

Choosing your channels

Now you need to take action to reach your priority targets and stakeholders. Let's start with looking at the obvious and maybe not so obvious choices of channels you have as an individual to market yourself.

STEP ONE

Decide how quickly you want to market yourself. How much time and effort can you motivate yourself to devote? You must be realistic here. Let yourself be guided by your intuition.

STEP TWO

Now, choose the suitable communication channels. Here are just a few examples. Be innovative!

- Writing e-mail and letters.
- Making personal calls.
- Making visits, having meetings.
- Arranging events.
- Arranging parties … then you'll also get invitations to others.
- Initiating activities and participating in others, getting yourself invited.
- PR activities: writing a book, writing articles.
- Taking part in discussions, politics, being active.
- Networking: finding networks, starting networks.

Do you have some other choices available?

STEP THREE

Install your activities in your future.

Let's use your timeline again, this time the future part. Try to make your own schedule of Brand Me activities by seeing in your mind when and how you will be doing certain things. The exact timing is not so crucial: it's more important that you see yourself doing all the things that you are planning. Make the images as detailed as possible.

Communicate at your own pace

To communicate change and to build your personal brand among other people takes action. Look at it like putting out seeds here and there. It never happens entirely by itself: once things get started they will run by themselves a little, but you will always have to inject energy into the process.

If people don't hear from you they assume that you are not interested. The effort you have to put in is to create a perception of attention and interest by simply keeping in touch.

The most important thing is that you must feel it's in your own interest to act. If you feel it's something forced on you, you'll never keep on.

If you don't feel at all moved to actively communicate your new Brand Me that's also OK, but in that case don't expect a quick implementation. It will take a while if you don't activate it yourself, but maybe you have the patience for that.

CASE STUDY Gradually completing the Brand Me Mind Space

Jacqueline

Anyone studying Jacqueline's curriculum vitae of the past 15 years would certainly be confused at first glance. 'Where is the strategy?' one would ask.

Having done some kind of fashion studies in her early twenties, she later worked in accounting, was a secretary, traded heavy machines, and then a few years ago, to the astonishment of her friends and family, she moved down to the south of France to be responsible for the southern European sales of a clothing manufacturer (without her French really being that good!).

Now, having decided that she wanted to learn something new and more demanding, she is studying chip programming and simultaneously working on a standardization project (Functional Dimension).

Well, what are her skills? What are her strong dimensions?

Taking a closer look and knowing more about her, we can give you a few hints. A sense for business and being good at calculation are probably things that help her, besides her being hardworking and dedicated to the job at hand. She has a strong Social Dimension, being imbued with something of a feminine mystique and softly spoken, and always keeping a curious attitude when meeting new people.

Maintaining this aptitude for learning and curiosity will probably keep her energy pointed in the right direction in the future also – whatever she does! She is gradually completing her Brand Me Mind Space.

part four
living Brand Me

07

chapter seven

job Brand Me – spin off a career

Individualism is now the name of the game – in society as well as in business. In 1989, the Berlin Wall – the emblem of collectivist shackles – crumbled and fell. Millions of people around the world watched on television, as people power was unleashed on the symbol of authoritarian rule.

In the eyes of many, it was a moment that defined a new world order – economic, political and social. Today, the internet is undermining that other collectivist power base, the corporation. Today, every one of us has to be a brand in our own right.

The importance of this has to do with you, but also with the group or network of which you are a part.

Paradoxically, we are now creating a new kind of collectivism, one based on individuality rather than conformity.

That's the crucial difference. Uniqueness is king. Against this background, the need to brand yourself and to know what you stand for is quite obvious. It makes it easier for you to find out where you fit in and how you will contribute to the group or network.

Who are you? Why are you different? What's your personality? How do you add value? These are the questions being asked by people who want to do business with you, employ you, or choose you as a member of a special project group. They are also questions we all ask ourselves from time to time, in fact they boil down to one of the most fundamental questions in human philosophy, the question of identity. In the old days you could always lean on other identities. The school or university you went to, for example, was a form of identity, especially if it was a well-known brand like Oxford or Harvard. Or it could be the company you worked for – you could identify yourself by referring to a big corporation: 'I'm an IBMer', or even 'I'm an ex-IBMer'.

But how helpful is that today? It might still be useful, but it is not decisive. We are less impressed by backgrounds than we used to be. What is really important now is the Brand Me. What *you are* is the most important factor in professional life. It is a much more democratic society. People have more equal chances, and young people can *be somebody* much faster.

To do something on your own, to achieve something, to build something with the talent you've got, that's what counts. Or put simply: what do you stand for? In the old days you could easily borrow some ideas to stand for, political, educational or social. Today it's more demanding. **You have to stand for something on your own**!

Work life used to be separate, but today it is likely to be far more integrated with your personal life. In both areas people demand to know who you are. The relationship we all want to have with other people is built on knowing, liking and accepting what they are in certain ways. It's when we don't know with whom we are dealing that we get uncomfortable, we begin to make our own hypotheses of what that person might be. The uncertainty makes us unsure and suspicious. Just as we don't like corporations that we can't trust because we don't know exactly what they stand for, the same applies to individuals. There are equally good reasons for human beings and corporations to stand for something. And in the transparent, online world in which we now live, this is increasingly important.

The purpose of this book is, of course, to bring clarity and insight to the individual's mind, but in the job context there's another purpose as well. Through a clearer understanding of your personal brand, you can gauge your fit with the corporate brand.

How do you fit the company you work for? And how does it fit you …?

If the company you work for doesn't fit you, you'd probably like to know. It's in your own interest, as much as your employer's, to understand how well you match your company. In today's recruitment market these are very important issues. To get the *right* kind of talent, to attract people, to match people to your business, are top management issues. It's not so different to making an acquisition of another company. In both cases you have to know what everyone stands for.

There are several good reasons for wanting a good brand fit between employee and employer:

- The brand is the core of the corporation; it's there for everybody to see.
- The same questions that define the brand can easily be used to define a person.
- People are one of the greatest assets in a modern business, and also the most important single asset in building a brand.

So to have one transparent value system for both the company as a whole and the individuals working for that company is as close to the entrepreneurial ideal of a brand as possible.

The brand is the differentiation code of the company as well as of the individual. Not that this means the individual should be exactly the same as the company (that is, unless you want an army of soldiers in uniform). The talents of individuals should complement the company, within the framework of the Brand Code. This is a common problem for every company when hiring talent:

if individuals are outside the company framework, it doesn't matter how talented they are!

Matching your brand with the brand of the company

The perfect tool to match your own brand with the brand of the company you work for, or are about to work for, is the Brand Code (or Brand Me Code for individuals). To use the Brand Code from a personal branding perspective, you start with the Brand Code of your company.

The company Brand Code

PRODUCT

What is the benefit for the customer?

POSITIONING

Why is our brand better than or different from those of the competitors?

STYLE

What characterizes the style of the brand, image, tonality, etc.?

Words or phrase, describing the main idea of the brand

MISSION

What is the brand's role in society, or the public benefit of the brand?

VISION

The brand can define its own future: in what market do we want to be?

VALUES

What makes the brand trustworthy as a friend?

If your company doesn't have one, you will have to construct one. To do that you need to read their websites, annual reports, corporate presentations and recruitment ads. You can also ask responsible people in the company specific questions in order to be able to fill in the six inputs: Product, Positioning, Style, Mission, Vision and Values. You might have to guess or estimate. You might also find an expression that could serve as the Brand Code Core Message (the Motto of the company).

Benefit

Looking at yourself as a 'product or service', you have to ask yourself what is the greatest benefit you bring to your organization? If your benefit and positioning, your competence and professionalism, are totally different from the company's product, then you seriously have to ask yourself what this means. Does it mean that you will be employed to complement the company, doing something that the company badly needs and currently lacks? If you are a true professional in your area, you will probably create respect and be beneficial. But it can also be a true mismatch. Ask yourself whether your ambitions in life are totally different or not from what this company's business seems to be. If you find that you are too far apart and think that they would not respect you for your speciality, then seek a job elsewhere.

Positioning

What is it that you do best? Why are you better than, or different from, others? And how does that fit with the positioning of the company in its market? Let's say that the company's positioning is to be different in the way it distributes its products and services its customers, and your difference is in being a very good researcher. Again, here a mismatch isn't necessarily negative, as long as the company appreciates the need for your expertise. But if it only needs people who do what the company is best at, and you don't want to position yourself like that, then you are in trouble here from Day One. On the other hand, if the company really needs you to deliver its difference, and you feel you will be valued for it, then it may be the right place for you.

To find out, you may have to check what your colleagues do, how they are positioned. This is usually easy to discover. Find out exactly what you are expected to do and in what context. Are there other people with similar sorts of positioning to yours that you will have to compete with? How do you rate your positioning in relation to them? Will you be valuable at all?

How would your differentiation help the company to differentiate?

That's the key question. If you are a very specialized and very good salesperson, your differentiation might do wonders for the company. If you feel you can do it, go for it. If you are doubtful, then look for a company where your specialization might be a better fit.

Style

When we talk about style, we mean the perception that you create – or want to create. It is more about the direct impression you make, your attitude and the feelings you create among others, whereas your deeper personality lies in your values.

Of course, it's good when your personal style fits well with the company culture. Ask yourself how much pain it would take for you to adjust. If you feel that merely minor adjustments are needed, then go for it.

Mission

The mission is about purpose and your role in society, or your benefit to the community. The company's mission may be one of your most important criteria for choosing an employer. If your own mission demands meaning and importance to humanity, then of course the company you work for should have the same leverage. This may come in stages and only ultimately produce the meaning you expect for yourself in life.

But be critical when you make such a judgement: do the managers really share a commitment to do what they say they will do? If they seem to stand behind their mission with commitment, but you yourself have a larger expectation, a more demanding and generous mission in your own Brand Me Code, it could still be OK. If on the other hand the company has a broader mission than your own, it may challenge your mission, which is great. Obviously the nature of the mission is important and should be in sync with yours.

If the company's mission totally fails to excite you, then your decision is easy, at least from a mission standpoint: you should not get involved.

Vision

See yourself 10–15 years from now. What picture comes to mind? Now do the same for your company. How well do the visions work together? A company with an exciting and large vision, larger than your own vision, but able to accommodate it, will present you with a good challenge. Try to find out if this big vision amounts to more than just words, if it has commitment and realism behind it.

If the company's vision is weak and your own vision stronger and larger, then beware.

A potential conflict awaits you down the line, but you might still consciously want to use this company as a stepping-stone in your career.

Note: Many companies use the expression 'mission' to describe their business idea or area. This is *not* our definition, as we discussed earlier. We see mission as a concept of role and responsibility in society. It's the business idea put in a larger context: how will the company contribute to the community or to mankind?

Values

These are usually the most important factor when matching your own brand with the brand of the company. Values are the rules of life, the deeper personality, the elements that will make the brand as trustworthy as a friend, and you as trustworthy as a good brand. You need to be careful here. Try to find out what the real values are; check and double check. If your own values clash with the values of the company, that should act as a warning.

The wording might be different, but the meaning is what counts. Some of your values might be missing and you may be able to live with that. But if some of the company's values are questionable, then you should definitely back out.

Conclusion

When you are matching your own Brand Me Code with the Brand Code of the company, you should pay particular attention to the items on the right-hand side: Mission, Vision, and Values. When it comes to Benefit / Product, Positioning and Style, a mismatch here can be fruitful and even necessary. If you are able to offer a different Benefit or Product to the company you work for, and have a different Positioning or competence, this might be exactly what is needed. A different Style might be refreshing. But if your own Mission, Vision and Values and those of the company are miles apart, then you will probably have trouble ahead.

How to choose your career

What drives you is a parallel question to 'What do you stand for?', the main question this book is set to answer. What drives you? The question assumes there is something, a force, a quest, a deep wish inside you, that subconsciously makes you do things and behave in a certain way.

A way of looking at this is to realize that you can have different strategies in life:

- To do professionally what you are most passionate about. This is the classical strategy of the **entrepreneur**.
- To do something to make it possible to do what you are most passionate about. In other words finding money and time to do what you really like, preferably in parallel. The risk with saving

The most important lesson we can learn from Richard's case is how important it is to follow your passion in life. It usually leads to success for three very important reasons. Firstly you seldom fail with something you are passionate about (you 'go with the flow') and you usually become very knowledgeable about what you are doing. Secondly it makes you less frustrated and all your energy is focused on one thing. Thirdly, and maybe most importantly, you are usually able to differentiate yourself and build a very strong personal brand.

Hugh Hefner – Playboy

Hugh Hefner, the founder of *Playboy*, is of course famous for his Social Dimension, his ability to create a social context around himself and the Playboy Mansion. Actors, politicians and businesspeople have always been on his guest list, and of course a

Hugh Hefner Brand Me Mind Space

FUNCTIONAL DIMENSION
Journalist, editor in chief and founder of *Playboy* magazine

SOCIAL DIMENSION
An extremely party-focused personality with a great ability to create a social context around himself and the Playboy Mansion, with actors, politicians and businesspeople on the guest list – and of course beautiful girls

BRAND ME MIND SPACE

MENTAL DIMENSION
Admired for his courage, integrity and ability to withstand a lot of pressure from the moral majority of the USA stretching the limits with elegance

SPIRITUAL DIMENSION
Fighting double standards

lot of attractive young women as well. Possibly Hefner has made some impact in the Spiritual Dimension with his liberal views on life and sex.

Find motivation by exploring your Brand Me Code

The life drive is usually a question of your **mission** in life. What do you believe in? What is the contribution you want to make to the community – in other words, your issue? It doesn't have to be that grand. Maybe your mission is not public at all: maybe it's for a small group of people with a close relationship, like your children, or the close community you live and work in. It could be helping unemployed people in your neighbourhood or helping an individual in need.

The other driving force for people as well as organizations is to have a **vision**. In other words, how will you be positioned in the future, or what does your dream image of yourself 10–15 years from now look like?

The third thing is the **values**. Do you have certain values that you really want to stand up for? A lot of people in our history have been driven by values such as freedom, democracy, equality and honesty, and they have got a lot of quality of life and satisfaction out of that. For some of us it's easier to relate to mission and vision as drivers, but of course these contain values anyway.

Times are changing, and the specific value drive is back in importance. Today we are very self-centred (egotistic, if you prefer), but humanity as a whole is moving towards higher ideals again.

A recommendation is to think about the implications of this for yourself, if you want to be ahead of the game. Ideals can definitely be part of a person's development. Ideals have traditionally been connected with rebellious young people, who feel they have a cause, even if sometimes it is a bit unclear and irrelevant. The older you get the more integrated your cause will be into your personality. It becomes a *mission* or your own special issue.

Personal development is about taking steps in life, from establishing your individuality and identity to becoming a part of society and becoming more unselfish and supportive of other people.

The Instant Motivator

This is a tool for increasing your motivation to do things which are valuable and important to you. For instance, do you wish you could get more motivated about your present work? Maybe you realize that it's good for you in many respects, if only you felt more motivated. Try this method.

STEP ONE

Sit back and relax. Think about your present work, or something else that you have a hard time enjoying, something you want to be more motivated to do.

STEP TWO

Now go through all the objections you feel when you think about carrying out your work or task. Listen carefully to your inner voice! For every objection that comes up, immediately think of something else which your inner self has no objection to. Be sure to go through all your objections!

STEP THREE

Think about the value of the work you have, what benefit you have from it, the financial as well as other benefits – think about the *end result* rather than the work process itself. How will you benefit from doing this work? What good feeling does it produce in the end?

STEP FOUR

Keep this good feeling in mind and imagine yourself doing the work you want to be more motivated to do. Now make it bigger, brighter, closer and more colourful. Add a good sound to the situation; hear positive, encouraging voices. Make the whole experience compelling and attractive and really motivating for you. Keep on doing this for a while until you feel positively attracted to your work.

Anita Roddick

The founder of Body Shop, simultaneously an entrepreneur and activist, Anita Roddick has both made a statement and differentiated herself from many other businesswomen and certainly from most businessmen.

The interesting and unusual thing about Anita Roddick is that she is a personal brand in her own right, not just as the founder of Body Shop. This is much due to the fact that she has an issue. To have an issue of public interest is of course always a good way of creating a strong personal brand.

Anita Roddick Brand Me Mind Space

FUNCTIONAL DIMENSION
A skilled businesswoman and activist who has built her differentiated Body Shop concept around ethics and a new way of thinking in business

SOCIAL DIMENSION
An enthusiastic, respected and straightforward person, admired for 'making sense'

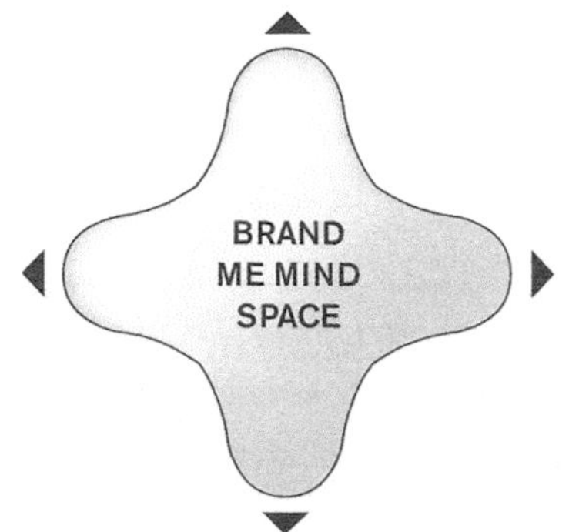

MENTAL DIMENSION
Inspires us to take global responsibility; a role model and inspiration for women to set up their own business and/or take action in an issue

SPIRITUAL DIMENSION
Driven by ethics and taking action: the environment, ethics in the workplace, being a good citizen productionwise, animal testing, etc.

08

chapter eight

team Brand Me – join your forces

Working in a team is a wonderful thing … when it works! But when it doesn't, it can create more problems than almost anything else in management.

That's why there is lots of literature available on teamwork and teambuilding. We have no intention of trying to bring something really new to this subject. On the contrary we will go back to some of the most obvious truths about teamwork, but show you how to use your newly acquired self-insights as a way of analyzing team members, whether they belong to a team you are already a part of, or are candidates for a team you are about to set up.

Team member matching

The most important thing in a team is finding your role, and of course making a contribution. The ideal team obviously consists of people with different talents, competences and personalities. At the same time this can mean problems: when the team members are so different, what is it that unites them?

Good leaders have a talent for inventing a culture, usually based on clear Mission, Vision and Values, that the members can then endorse as their own. The more different the members are, the more talented in different ways and the stronger their personalities (and in creative teams this can be extremely strong), the more powerful the culture has to be.

In other words, in team building there are three important tasks:

1 Clearly define the expected outcome of the teamwork.

2 Find the right combination of members to successfully fulfil the assignment.

3 Create a unifying, productive culture.

The very first thing is establishing what the outcome of the teamwork should be. It almost goes without saying: the more clearly you can define the expected result, the better off you are.

The next thing is to scout around and recruit the right people. This can be very difficult if you are searching for very special people and have little experience or no network in a particular area. But it can also be easy, if you have done similar things before. Many teams are routinely formed from people who know each other or have worked together successfully before, but that is not necessarily a guarantee that it will work this next time around too.

Maybe you should be more daring about trying some new groupings.

If you want a way to know more about new team members and how they could possibly work together successfully, the Brand Me method can be of tremendous help.

After doing the Brand Me process with yourself you know a lot more about what you stand for as a person. Now imagine that the prospective team members of your new team have also done the same process; imagine that they all know their Mottos and have their Brand Me Code. Imagine that you then sit down and talk about how you match each other based on that information.

Maybe it is unrealistic to ask everyone in your team to do the Brand Me process described in this book.

The next best thing you can do is to interview everybody using the Brand Me Code as a guide. And furthermore you could actually create a Team Brand Code. At the end of this chapter we have a format for a workshop for your team to do this together; it works well as a first test on teamwork too.

When you are interviewing your prospective team members, here is what to look for.

The left-hand side of the Brand Me Code is the 'practical' side. From here you can get an idea of how well the team members will complement each other in skill sets and experiences, and also in their outer styling.

On the right-hand side of the Brand Me Code you find the elements of the culture that will bond the team members.

Benefit

Ask the candidate what they perceive to be their personal key benefit for the team. This of course will give an indication of the skill set that the person has, and you can then match it with the different skills needed in the team. The interesting thing with questions about Benefit is that they imply an answer based on the self-perceived benefit, not necessarily the formal skills and training that the person has.

Positioning

If you ask the candidate what makes them different and better than others in the team situation, you will provoke them to be different. This is of course good, because you may find out about some special skills or experiences that can be of great value for the team.

Style

Ask the candidate what their key traits as a person in the team situation are. Here you have the possibility to touch on the sort of things that can be tricky in a normal interview situation, such as personal behaviour and style. If you have the Team Brand Code it's easy to compare your candidate's answer with the style the other members have set.

Mission

In order to figure out how motivated a person will become in the team it's good to find out something about that person's own idea of a mission. Is it something that is at all in line with the Team Mission? If not, is it totally obstructive to the Team Mission?

Vision

Same thing goes for Vision. What personal vision does this candidate have? Is it at all in sync with the Team Vision? Does the personal vision embrace the Team Vision? If not, does it obstruct it?

Values

Values in a team are very much like the code of conduct between the members, but they're also a part of the team culture. It is interesting to find out if the person's own values are at all aligned with the Team Values. Start by asking the candidate about their values; then explain the Team Values. Then ask the candidate again how well aligned they feel with the other team members. If the answer is not at all, watch out!

The team as culture within a culture

One company, one brand, one message is of course what most companies strive for. If you study the history of some of the larger corporations it's striking to see how small teams of people have experimented with new ways of doing things that have later led to the development of the whole business area, and even led to the survival of the whole company. These kinds of teams are simply essential for innovation in bigger organizations.

Of course the problem with a very strong corporate culture is that it can kill everything that is not aligned with it.

To be successful, most companies have to find a way to balance this, to be able to create cultures within cultures, team cultures that motivate innovative people to stay with the team and help to re-create the whole organization. If you have a problem with balance, using branding as a process can be a very good way of handling the situation.

Let's take an example.

Several years ago we worked on this with one of the largest international and Scandinavian-based companies. The problem was that their main culture, products and brand at that time were geared to a traditional customer segment that was totally different to an emerging new kind of customer with other values and attitudes. A team of people was recruited, mostly from inside this big corporation, to work with this new segment, creating new products but also, as a side-effect, creating a culture that was totally different.

The team came to ask us for help with creating an internal brand – a special team brand – that is, a culture within a culture. They felt they had to attract the right people internally, but even more so to be accepted in the new market. When we did the team branding in a workshop together with the whole team, we still carefully tied the new virtual sub-brand (they still used the same logo and so on as the main organization) to the corporate brand, but they had their own Motto and many parts of the Team Brand Code were different.

The transparent three-level branding system

A good way to handle the situation of doing three things at once – developing and matching the right individuals as team members, creating a motivated team and still remaining aligned with the brand of the corporation as a whole – is to use the same branding system transparently throughout. Our branding methodology, being very fundamental and easy to use, provides this transparency; you are able to use the same basic tools for all the three levels of branding, individual, team and corporate.

The transparent three-level branding system

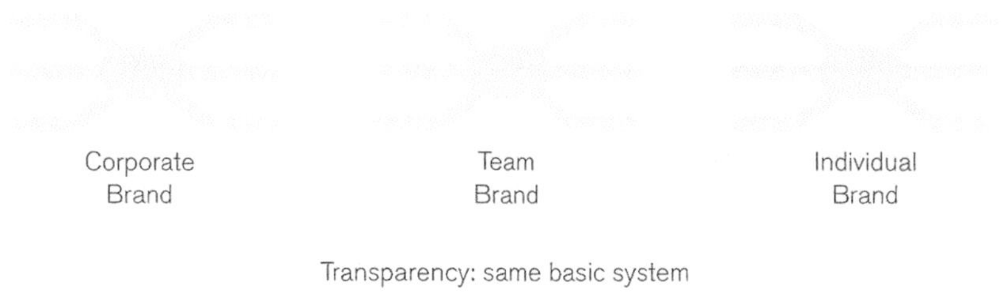

Corporate
Brand

Team
Brand

Individual
Brand

Transparency: same basic system

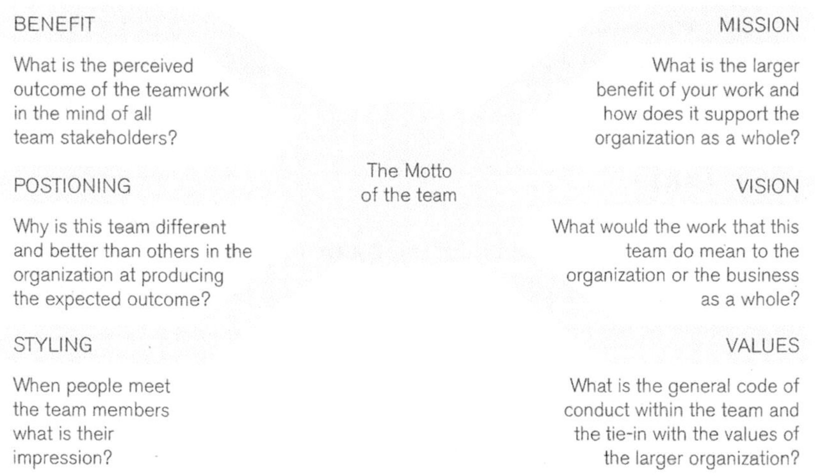

The Motto
of the team

BENEFIT

What is the perceived outcome of the teamwork in the mind of all team stakeholders?

POSTIONING

Why is this team different and better than others in the organization at producing the expected outcome?

STYLING

When people meet the team members what is their impression?

MISSION

What is the larger benefit of your work and how does it support the organization as a whole?

VISION

What would the work that this team do mean to the organization or the business as a whole?

VALUES

What is the general code of conduct within the team and the tie-in with the values of the larger organization?

The Team Brand Workshop

This is an excellent way to start your teamwork. It does several things for your team: it creates a culture and a context for everybody to feel a part of, and it connects to the larger organization of which the team is a part. But the most important thing is that it gives all team members a sync that is very valuable. Everyone in the team will feel an ownership in setting out what the team should stand for, and that means they can deliver much more energy in the teamwork to follow. ▶

STEP ONE

Decide to create a Team Brand Code! You do this by using the same format as the Brand Me Code but instead you are looking at it as if the whole team were one person or shared one mind.

STEP TWO

Start with the **Benefit of the teamwork**. Here you try to describe the outcome of the teamwork as well as you can. Again, think about the outcome anticipated by the people you are reporting to, and by the stakeholders of the team (it may be slightly different from the formal task).

STEP THREE

Then move on to **Positioning of the team**. Again, try to describe as clearly as possible why the team is different and likely to be better than others in the organization at producing the expected outcome you have set in Step One. Also try to sense how this positioning fits in with the positioning in the marketplace for the larger organization.

STEP FOUR

Now define the **Style of the team**, as if it were a company of its own. When people meet your team members what impression do they form? Do you have any symbols or rituals or a special language? Style is the outer marker of your team culture! How does yours sync with the style of the organization as a whole?

STEP FIVE

It's time to go one step deeper into your special team culture: what is your **Mission?** What is the larger benefit of your work? And more important: how does it **support the organization or corporation as a whole**, and how will it help the organization deliver its overall Mission? It's important to sync well with the master organization; team success is always measured in those terms.

STEP SIX

The **Vision of the team** is a very motivating factor for the team members; it's the key mental picture that everyone carries and that bonds together people with very different backgrounds, skills and experiences. Imagine a few years ahead: **what will the work that this team does mean to the organization or the business as a whole?** A successful team within an organization can save the life of the whole body, or pave the way for a new strategy. But it has to be endorsed by it: the link has to be there.

STEP SEVEN

The **Values of the team** should tie in with the values of the organization it's a part of, but they should also comprise the rules that make things work between the members. It's very good to have these as a general code of conduct within the team.

STEP EIGHT

Finally, creating the **Motto for the team** – a one-liner – is a good way to join the forces in the team together. It's also a fun thing to do as a group activity, and having a Motto for the team in the first place always impresses other people.

Teams of talents

Teams are essential in all businesses, not least in the entertainment business. We all know about film teams, set up for a specific film production, for a limited time and with a selected group of specialists who after the job is done scatter and move on to new productions in new formations.

In the music industry the teams are the bands, and if one studies these it's obvious how well they are composed to produce an outcome that is larger than the sum total of what each member could produce. Bands in music are usually formed spontaneously, and when a member leaves for one reason or another the magic in the music produced often disappears. Also when members of a band start their own career it is usually a disappointment: it doesn't reach the same magic, even when they were the leading artists in their bands. Maybe they sometimes realize that they needed the band more than they liked to admit, but too late. For many successful bands the reunion has become a trend, even though everybody knows it's not going to be like it was in their heyday.

A lesson from this for all teams is that a team has its time. When it has reached its peak performance, it's good to dissolve and form new constellations.

Let's look at the composition of three music teams in terms of the Brand Me Mind Space of the members.

The Beatles

The Beatles are a good example of how a team can successfully combine different personalities. Paul McCartney and John Lennon are definitely the strongest of the Beatle personalities.

Paul is not only a good musician, something he has developed over the years (Functional Dimension), but also a very good-hearted and sociable person with a developed Social Dimension.

John Lennon was, of course, equally well known for his Spiritual Dimension, being an activist who focused world attention on peace and freedom. He also had a Mental Dimension, being a powerful mentor for a lot of people, inspiring them to express their feelings and consciousness. Obviously his Functional Dimension was as a musician and songwriter. John Lennon had a truly four-dimensional character.

Other examples

Bono has described the composition of U2 in terms of the base player Adam Clayton and the drummer Larry Mullen as the two legs, the foundation in the band; the guitar player, The Edge, as the brain; and Bono himself as the heart. Of course they all need each other to be able to give a complete performance.

Bono is himself also an example of a multidimensional public person. He has become this partly through being the spokesperson for U2 and partly because of his own way of expressing himself. He is also the most outgoing and charismatic personality in the band.

Simon and Garfunkel never became the same success as individual performers that they were together, when their personalities balanced each other perfectly.

Sometimes it's really impossible for one person to do what a well-formed band can do together. By using a good knowledge of what each member stands for and contributes, i.e. by having developed Brand Me, you as a leader are able to compose the perfect band for your project.

09

chapter nine
leader Brand Me – go ahead and do it

As a leader the first thing you have to know is yourself. With your Brand Me Code you are equipped with more self-knowledge than most leaders. In fact, lacking self-insight is one of the largest problems in the area of leadership.

As a leader you are supposed to have a **vision**, to be able to see ahead and take your subordinates on a route into a successful future. But your own vision of yourself might not be enough to lead a whole organization. That's why it's so important that you as a leader build a brand platform for your company as well as yourself, if somebody else hasn't done it already. Try to look at your platform with the perspective that the Brand Me process has given you.

Rather than waiting for your top management to become motivated by such an idea, it's important to make a start yourself, where you are, at your department level.

This exercise will be your first important step as a Brand Me Leader. You will share and involve your own people in the key strategy for your unit, also assessing the strategy for the company as a whole. There is nothing more motivating for people.

To motivate and to recruit people, you will as a Brand Me Leader put your emphasis on the **mission**, the reason for people to go to work and feel good about it. Here we are talking about the corporate mission, the role your company plays in society or the company issue. But it is also important to synchronize your own mission with the corporate one. A leader who is in sync with the mission of the company, or at least not in conflict with it, is usually a good leader. In Chapter 7 we have already discussed synchronization between corporate Brand Code and personal Brand Me Code.

Tony Blair

Tony Blair is definitely a politician worth studying from a branding point of view. He is relatively young and has a strong Spiritual Dimension: to create a modern Britain. He has the energy and will to make decisions – and to act. Accomplishing this in his position takes quite a large Social Dimension, making people around him enthusiastic about, or at least supportive of, the idea or project in question.

Tony Blair Brand Me Mind Space

FUNCTIONAL DIMENSION
A bold leader and prime minister who dares to make decisions not appreciated by everyone and take action also in controversial issues (and gets away with it)

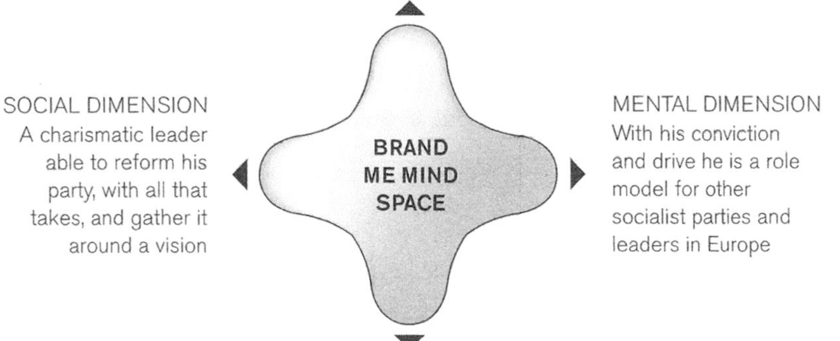
SOCIAL DIMENSION
A charismatic leader able to reform his party, with all that takes, and gather it around a vision
BRAND ME MIND SPACE
MENTAL DIMENSION
With his conviction and drive he is a role model for other socialist parties and leaders in Europe

SPIRITUAL DIMENSION
The vision to create a modern Britain

The five steps to becoming a Brand Me leader

1. It's all about energy and being able to transfer energy to others with enthusiasm.

Use your Brand Me Code to get inspired and communicate yourself.

2. Being able to transfer passion to others has a lot to do with being a charismatic person.

Charisma is, as we discussed earlier, about alignment, which creates attraction, drive, persuasion and inspiration. To some degree it's a talent, but it's also largely a matter of technique. See 'Enhance your charisma' in Part Two, Chapter 3. It's about consciously setting out to be a role model for other people, which in turn is about unlocking other people's energy and talent.

How do you do this when you don't feel the passion?

There are two ways to handle this:

- Try to find a new angle to the task. See the Instant Motivator in Part Four, Chapter 7. Maybe you could see the task as a stepping-stone in your development, something integrated in your own plan.
- If this doesn't work at all, find something else to do which gives you more passion. But soon!

Charismatic leadership advice

1. Give of yourself. Be generous and inviting about who you are, without fear. The less you fear, the more confident you will be perceived to be.
2. Be attentive. Listen to others and refer to them in your communication.
3. Have a positive attitude. See everybody as a possibility, and mistakes as learning opportunities and indications.
4. Be curious. Show an interest in different aspects of life.

5 Use visual language. This will encourage people to see for themselves. You don't have to be detailed, though: give space for their own imagination. Use metaphors and stories when explaining.

6 Share your experiences. Make these stories your own as much as possible. Use your own experiences and elaborate. Dare to be personal!

7 Always integrate and involve. Empower! Dare to take chances by giving your team opportunities. Delegate!

8 Have fun together. Be less formal and more of a friend. Your team knows that you are the boss anyway, because you are in charge.

3. Composing the right team

Doing a branding workshop with your team, as discussed in Part Four, Chapter 8, is an excellent way of starting off as a team leader. It's a good way to test the team interaction and at the same time involve all the team members in setting the culture of the team.

4. Motivating the team

The best way of motivating the team is to take the Corporate Brand Code (if there isn't one you may have to construct it based on the Brand Code format), and then try to integrate it in the daily work of everybody in the team. The problem with a lot of strategic stuff in a company is that it stays strategic and is never filtered down to where the action is. 'What does the Brand Code mean in my work?' is the crucial question. And 'How does it affect my decisions and performance?'

This exercise can be done easily. First you divide into sub-teams if your team is larger than five people. Two to three members in each sub-team is ideal, preferably representing a mix of different job tasks and backgrounds.

Then we recommend you to use the Brand Me Activity Generator. Give each sub-team the full Brand Code. Then put the Brand Code Motto of the company (or the team) in the centre. Ask everybody to think in the four dimensions about how they could use the Corporate Brand Code in their work, and contribute to the success of the company.

They should think in practical terms about this, focusing on real activities or ways of doing things. When they do it they should try to think of all the different stakeholders: customers, fellow employees (not forgetting the internal market of services to others), public opinion and the owners.

5. Follow-up on team members

It's a brilliant idea to use the Corporate Brand Code as a platform for any follow-up and evaluation meetings with each individual. It's an efficient tool for evaluation, since it's the company goals and not your own. It's quality control, if you like, for each team member and for the contribution of the team as a whole. Using the same format you can check how each member is aligned with the Corporate Brand Code and how he or she is contributing to the corporate result. You can also check how each member is interacting with the group.

Practically you start with **Product/Benefit** in the Corporate Code and discuss how the team member contributes to this. Is the team member satisfied and are you as a leader satisfied? Here is of course an excellent opportunity for both honest criticism and appreciation.

Under **Positioning** there is an opportunity to talk about the team member's relationship with and role within the team. In addition, you can also talk about how the individual has contributed to the company positioning in the marketplace. It may seem far-fetched for some, but put into perspective it's important for everyone's work to be connected to the market situation of the company as a whole.

Let the team member comment on anything in the **Style** that they find difficult, also how they have been able to take part in its development.

Under **Mission** you have an opportunity to discuss how well this is aligned with the individual. Don't forget to ask the individual member about his or her own mission, or maybe passion in life.

It is important to identify with the **Vision** of the company. Try to check how it motivates each individual.

And last the **Values**. How has the individual lived up to the company values? Are some of them difficult to understand? This is a good opportunity to discuss it.

There may also be situations on the job that go against the values.

Try to talk about these things. The effect is that the company values will then become clearer and more important, not just words on a paper. You are now embarking on a value-based conversation with your team, which is the true starting point for high motivation and top performance.

Sven-Göran Eriksson, the wizard coach

To choose a Swedish coach for the English national football team is a bold thing to do. Many were the voices rising in opposition: a foreigner?

Luckily for the team – and for himself – Eriksson is a mentally strong person who is able to coach himself as well as the team. So when given the England appointment he got straight down to work. Soon enough the team was achieving good results ... and a few months later even better results. What secrets does this foreigner have to hand?

Well, 'None', he would probably say himself, being a calm, no-nonsense man. But we know that he believes strongly in mental coaching (having also co-written a book with an authority in the field), and is able to develop each team member's inner strengths and make them see the vision. The fact that he is a mentor with a non-hierarchal attitude toward team formation demonstrates his social qualities. Eriksson has the ability to bring the team together and maintain a positive but low-key attitude himself, even though he gets a lot of personal attention in the media.

His passion for football has been there since early childhood, and it has of course helped him along the way. But we must also remember that his actual skills have played an important part, e.g. his ability to strategically put the individual players together – in a position where the team is getting the best out of each player. The result has been several championship and cup wins over the years for his teams.

And the Spiritual Dimension? Well, of course there must be a strong vision of taking the team in question to new heights. But what has also come out of his success with the England team is that corporate management and media are now taking a closer look at him and his Swedish management style, a style based upon a non-hierarchal consensus-oriented attitude and empowerment. Although empowerment in the workplace has been talked about in Britain and America for many years, Eriksson seems to fuel the process by his results.

Sven-Göran Eriksson Brand Me Mind Space

FUNCTIONAL DIMENSION
Has an ability to strategically put the individual players together – in a position where the team is getting the best out of each player

SOCIAL DIMENSION
Holds the team together by his non-hierarchal attitude; low-key himself, even though he personally gets a lot of media attention

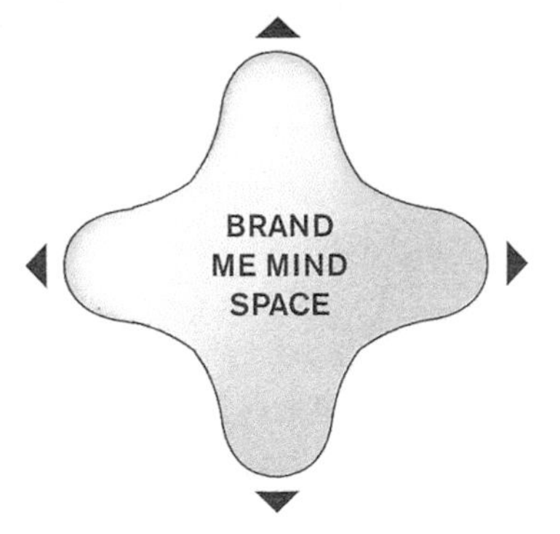

MENTAL DIMENSION
Coaches the team members' inner strengths and makes them see the vision; a role model for corporate management

SPIRITUAL DIMENSION
Empowers individuals to form a strong team; demonstrates an efficient, empowered leadership style

10

chapter ten

relationship Brand Me – make a better match

This is the philosophy-of-life aspect of Brand Me. 'If I know more about myself I will be more interesting for others to know, and I will know consciously how better to relate to others.' This is the essence of how you can use your Brand Me to guide your life as a social being.

It's true that in the end you have to make your own experiences. But having a Brand Me Code to fall back on will put your experiences with other people in context with yourself. At least you will have something to hold on to if a crisis appears: a broken relationship or deceptive behaviour by someone you regard as your friend. One way to clarify your relationship for yourself and your partner is to match your Brand Me Code with theirs. But remember: if you start looking for the perfect match you may either give up or become very cynical.

Have you ever found yourself saying, 'He (or she) is exactly my type' about a new object of attraction? Since we are all pre-programmed with images of our ideal partner this is quite common. But how often we are mistaken when we think we have met Mr(s) Right. The reason for this is that initially we are looking at the more obvious parts of the partner's personality, usually the left-hand side of the Brand Me Code: Benefit – their job or education; Positioning – their social environment; and Style – the traits of the person that catch the eye.

Have you ever experimented with trying to really get to know someone who is not 'your type', and stayed with the idea long enough to be able to find out whether or not they are?

Or maybe you have met a person, let's say at work, and done just the same: you became friends first and then gradually found that an attraction suddenly appeared. What you have experienced then is being able, without being blocked by your pre-programmed ideal, to investigate the right-hand side of that person's Brand Me Code: Mission – being fascinated by the person's passion or drive to do certain things is a great start; Vision – their ideas of where they want to go in life can be very seductive; and also you may have, as part of the 'friendship game' rather than 'lovers' game', been able to find out what this person really stands for – their Values.

Partner matching

Let's look in more detail into how you can use your Brand Me Code and that of your partner to test the matching potential in a relationship. But how do you do this without having your partner's Brand Me Code? One way is to simulate it for your partner, guessing and estimating their characteristics. This has its weaknesses, since you may not see the more interesting subtleties of their personality. A better way is to do the Brand Me workshop together as an activity to learn to know each other better.

In terms of a relationship, the most important parts of the code to match well are Style, Mission and Values.

Benefit and Positioning may connect more to your professional life. It's less sensitive for the two people in a relationship to have different talents; it may, on the contrary, be positively beneficial, even interesting for your relationship. It only becomes a problem when your talent and your professional life include a style that you don't share with your partner. Maybe you are into farming and your partner hates the idea of living in the countryside.

Style is definitely something you have to look into closely, because even if it may seem shallow, quite often it puts you into a social context that indirectly affects values. For example, if your partner is madly into hip-hop you have to accept the values of the hip-hop culture.

Mission, on the other hand, is something that it is great to have in common. In fact, relationships are mostly about sharing something in a more profound way. Having the same beliefs and sense of urgency will make your relationship less vulnerable to the trivialities of everyday life. To share a Spiritual Dimension is therefore a powerful matchmaker. If your partner has an issue that is totally uninteresting to you, be wary. Sooner or later you have a conflict coming, when you will need to choose your priorities for how you spend your time and money and where you want to live and work, etc. A checkpoint is: do I respect the other person's mission? You don't need to share it, but you must respect it and support it, at least passively.

To have no mission at all in life can be a potential attraction builder, since you can hook on to your partner's mission. A person who has a strong mission is usually both attractive and interesting. The risk is that you can become absorbed in something that you later realize is not your own conviction.

To share a **Vision** is more complicated. The kind of vision that relates to a person's work life can be difficult to share, but a vision about life in general, where and how to live, the role of family, the sort of friends and activities you want, and so on, is obviously very important to have in common. If you share a strong future joint vision it will be a driving force for the relationship.

The benefit of using the Brand Me methodology is that it enables you to start a conversation with each other and to use a common language as an idea platform for reaching beyond assumptions, interpretations and clichés.

Maybe **Values** are the most important things to share in relationships. At the same time this is the most difficult area, simply because values have to be described in words and interpreted emotionally. A lot of subtleties of definition will get in the way of this process.

To handle that, you have to use examples. Put the values into practical situations, relating them to things that you have both experienced. Prepare for a much longer and more complicated session in this area than in the others. It may even be impossible to talk about values together, because of the sensitivity and difficulty of the matter.

If the values you are discussing sound like no more than words that may feel lifeless generalizations, please refrain from analyzing the words themselves and let them be a subject for subconscious interaction. Put the values in your everyday life: what consequences would they have? The fact that you both get to this insight starts the subconscious process. The subconscious is given the order to work on it.

An objection that may arise when talking about transparency in relationships is that openness destroys intimacy and mystique. If you feel it's difficult to talk about values, then leave the matter entirely to your subconscious minds.

Relationships over time

In a relationship you also tend to influence each other in many different ways; you sync with the other person as a part of the intimacy. When you first fall in love this is quite OK: it's a part of being absorbed by each other. With time you may find it threatening to your own integrity as a person. But if you have the same basic values and maybe a joint mission or even vision to share, then together you are into something larger than both of you individually. One plus one becomes three, and your feeling of integrity loss is no longer relevant.

Typically in a relationship you will not notice your differences in the first five years. In the first months you will even attribute your own values to your partner in a wish for perfection, totally seduced by the miracle that you two of all people met in the first place.

After five years or so you will begin first to notice, then maybe to be irritated by, the mismatch in values. You will get a feeling of a lack of deep understanding, sense something is profoundly wrong in your relationship.

Women in these situations tend to become tougher and more active. They will try to change the man, or at least play with the idea of doing so. Of course this will further dramatize the situation and make matters worse. The moment you feel that your partner is not basically accepting you for what you are, the trust of the relationship is killed. 'Am I not good enough?' is a hard thought to take for most of us, especially if we have lived in a relationship for a long time, and have many years of shared history.

If, for example, a socially established woman falls madly in love with a wild rock musician, she will at first be absorbed by the love itself, excited by his lifestyle: it's new, different and challenging. But soon she will put this relationship into the context of the other people she knows, and start consciously or subconsciously to match values.

If you have a strong position in your social context, you might enjoy demonstrating your power by daring to challenge its values. But most of us haven't got that dominant position among our friends and family. We feel that we need social acceptance.

Your closest friends are more accepting if you do something different. They might shake their heads, but they will know if and when you feel good about acting a little rebelliously. They will also help you when something goes wrong, when you are going completely off track, and when you show signs of feeling bad they may come to your rescue.

The patience of your friends with a new partner of yours can be quite extensive, but in the end any dislike they feel will manifest itself, and that's when you yourself begin to doubt your relationship. You might want to fight for it for a while. But after the first passion has died the values of your friends generally become more important, and that's natural.

Sometimes, however, it can prove necessary to leave behind your friends' values.

You may not truly share them; the authentic *you* may have other values. In these circumstances, how should you go about making the change?

Consider first whether the differences between the values of your friends or family and those of your partner really are so large. Your friends' judgement may be based on superficial observations of style, and their lack of deeper experience of your partner may result in an incorrect perception of his or her values.

Values always need a long time to be proven; a track record has to be established. When time has passed, your group may re-evaluate your partner and find that there is no value mismatch at all. 'He is actually rather nice' may be your friends' surprised comment.

If you decide to truly break out of your social context anyway, then you have to be prepared to stand up for your actions and accept their consequences, even gather strength from the situation itself. You are pursuing true rebellion; you only have to be sure of the profoundness of your new cause.

Is your cause real, or is it pure tactics on your part or just revenge of some kind? If it's either of the latter two, you can still go ahead, but you should accept that it might not be forever.

In cases like this it's sometimes a relief to look at life as a series of projects, where nothing lasts forever: it's just something you do for a while, and then you do something else.

Quite a few of us have experience of this kind of value rebellion. But we also have experience of returning to our old values more or less voluntarily.

Ingmar Bergman

Ingmar Bergman is perhaps the most controversial among classic film makers, being both a film and theatre director, and also a scriptwriter and the creator of films like *The Seventh Seal*, *Persona* and *Scenes from a Marriage* and numerous productions of classic plays by such authors as Molière, Strindberg and Shakespeare.

He is functionally a very productive person, and works several hours a day writing scripts and creating new work. In 2001 he was still active: after having done only stagework for a few years, he started doing film and a TV follow-up to his famous *Scenes from a Marriage*, at the age of 83.

His Social Dimension is next to non-existent in his private life, but when working in the theatre or with film he is a charismatic director and presenter of his work. He creates a strong social context with the actors and the film or theatre crew. He refuses all kinds of public social life.

Bergman's Mental Dimension is as strong as his Functional: he has dedicated his life to personal inner exploration and development, and created a unique art of deep psychological drama. He has mentored many actors (Liv Ullman is just one of them), inspiring them to get the most out of themselves. He has also inspired many film makers and a lot of people in the audience to think about film and life in a different and more profound way.

The Spiritual Dimension of Ingmar Bergman is all about his mission from the very outset of his career to develop and make films and theatre in an entirely new way, as mental and psychoanalytical drama. Thus he has challenged a lot of stereotypes and clichés and contributed substantially to the development of film making.

Ingmar Bergman Brand Me Mind Space

FUNCTIONAL DIMENSION
Extremely talented and skilled scriptwriter, director and dramatizer both for cinema and for the stage; a perfectionist and very persistent

SOCIAL DIMENSION
Privately almost asocial, he has a great way of communicating with actors and is very respected and admired by creative talent; he inspires an intellectual but vivid community of film makers and fans

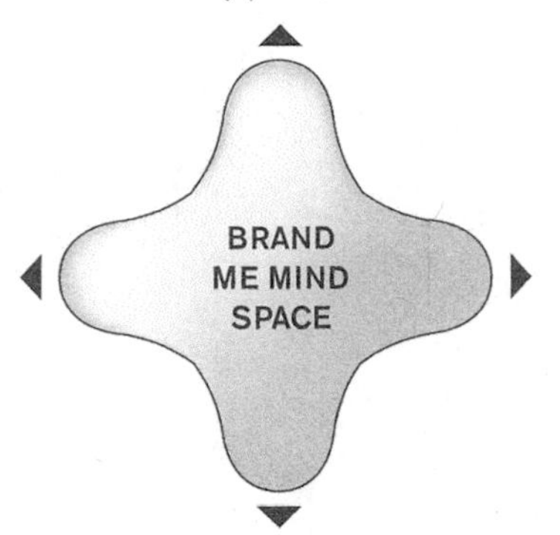

MENTAL DIMENSION
Has dedicated his life to personal inner exploration and development and has also mentored many actors and inspired a lot of people in the audience to think about life in a more profound way

SPIRITUAL DIMENSION
His mission was from the outset to develop and make films in an entirely new way, as an inner mental and psychoanalytical drama

part five
future Brand Me

11

chapter eleven

buyer Brand Me – give the right signals in the marketplace

We live in the time of the organized consumer. Marketing is now changing dramatically from being extremely seller-centric – a push marketing, a mass marketing, a stimuli-and-response marketing – to a pull marketing, a one-to-one marketing, where the well-informed customer or buyer is in charge.

Why was marketing originally so narcissistic and seller-centric? There's a historical reason for this, but it's also a question of the cost of information, and who controls it. It's about industrialism in the 1950s, when an overproduction of goods needed marketing to create consumer demand, and thus marketing and the media became almost as powerful as the industry they were to serve. In addition it was only the larger corporations that could afford to collect, process and communicate marketing information. And as a result of seller-centric marketing, the cost of going to market rose: on average for consumer products this eats up at least 50% of total costs.

'Would you be prepared to buy the marketing as the consumer?' That is a very real question. 'And even if a product is not better, the seller still makes the consumer believe that,' says marketing journalist Alan Mitchell, who in his book *Right Side Up* explains why and how seller-centric marketing is now dramatically turning into buyer-centric: 'The answer is mostly "no", the only marketing we will like to pay for is for new innovations, and maybe also for the "tell-me" or "educate-me" kind of marketing that we need in order to be better buyers.'

The driver of this change is of course the internet: what commercial TV was for the era of seller-centric mass marketing, the internet is becoming for the new era of buyer-centric one-to-one marketing.

It's shifting the information power from the big corporations to each individual, or to the 'consumers', as we are known in the arrogant and cynical power vocabulary of seller-centric marketers.

And we are not talking about the collective buying power that consumers have harnessed in some countries by banding together in co-operatives. We are talking about millions of consumers individually becoming as savvy as professional buyers in comparing price, performance and quality of everything from goods and services to knowledge, entertainment and information.

We are also talking about a new activist consumer movement, with books like Naomi Klein's *No Logo* and the almost militant internet movement The Cluetrain Manifesto addressing the tone of voice and arrogance of big corporations when they talk 'down' to us consumers.

Consumers have always done marketing

There is nothing new about this. Consumers and buyers have always compared the prices and quality of goods and services. Haggling about prices at market stalls is as old as trade itself.

The problem is that in modern life, time has become more precious than anything else.

Already today the value of all the time spent by consumers doing marketing – comparing, selecting, deciding on and actually buying services and in addition transporting goods – is considerable. If it were recalculated and priced like work, it would be more valuable than the combined cost of all seller-centric marketing, estimates Alan Mitchell. We are constantly struggling to share our time between all those activities that we have to do and those we like doing. For most people there is simply very little time for being a buyer; that's why we have accepted 'buying' marketing from the sellers.

For example by choosing a particular brand for a commodity I as a buyer save time, and have some control, or at least I feel I do, over the quality. I know I have to pay extra for this brand but I have to date accepted the fact because my time is so valuable and there were no real alternatives until recently.

But now that information about what I want to buy is easier to access and cheaper, in fact almost free, I have the possibility to take on a new active role as buyer. But the problem with time (and generating personal interest in the buying process) is still a problem for me!

Introducing the buyer agent

For a seller to use an agent to simplify the *selling* process is nothing new. We are used to turning to an agent if we want to sell our house, for instance.

But to use an agent for *buying* is fairly unusual, at least for everyday things and commodities. But an agent is really what we need in order to make our buying more efficient – to save time and labour. An agent not only for actual buying, but to find the right solutions for our needs in a wider sense, the right knowledge and the right kind of entertainment that we really enjoy.

Most of the agents helping us today appear on the surface to be paid by the sellers. For example a bank trying to sell us savings usually acts as a broker of funds and gets paid by a provision from the treasurer of the fund. But what's sure is that we as savers will have to pay the cost in the end, even though we don't have the benefit of choosing how much. The point is we are actually marketed to and have to pay the costs for this marketing.

Now, with the shift of information power and the easy access to information, everything is changing to our advantage. It means in effect that we buyers will gradually become more and more powerful in the marketplace. Provided that we can get organized, or get some help getting organized, and use this advantage, things can become quite interesting!

Who can help us consumers to 'align' to the sellers in a way that really cuts costs and saves time and labour? That would be a real win–win system instead of the present seller-centric lose–lose one, and in the end would produce more value … and more wealth!

What we need is someone who can make the offers in the marketplace more comprehensive and more comparable. And of course there are plenty of willing enterprises offering to help us consumers by doing just that.

Many of these are of course strictly internet based, since the internet and the information flow on it are the reason for change in the first place. An interesting point here is that those seller-centric organizations trying to adapt to the buyer-centric situation will have an excellent chance to develop their business and get it out of the rut where many feel they have got stuck.

A new era of branding

When marketing turns right side up, when the buyer takes on the role as driver in any business, then of course the concept of 'branding' has to change. Today most of the brands are very seller-centric, and terribly narcissistic; all market research is nervously asking, 'What does the consumer think of us?'

Now, the new power buyer shouts, 'I want to be a brand!'

It may sound weird in a way, but the branding of tomorrow is not at all exclusively for sellers: buyers will become strong brands by declaring what they stand for! What we want is a manifestation in the marketplace, just as some people buy themselves personal number plates for their cars or set up a personal web page.

Maybe we will not all be such narcissists as to do our branding individually to that extent. Many of us will make our voice heard in the marketplace by creating clubs or becoming members in existing communities or buyer groups that will act as our branding agents, or solution agents.

The brands will be part of our personal network, just like friends, being sources of information, support, reference and evaluation. 'Brands' will not just be companies, products and services. They will also be people, 'thought-schools', trends, culture and technologies, etc. All of us need to build ourselves a 'network brand' in order to establish our identity (see more about this in Chapter 12, 'Real Brand Me'), and some commercial brands will assist us in doing this!

A new definition of what branding is all about is needed

Here's a suggestion: 'Branding is about developing relationships which people value.' The goal for any business in the new buyer-centric era will be to create a win–win value exchange between the seller and the buyer, with as little loss and inefficiency as possible. Nobody will want to pay for the marketing in the future.

Personal branding becomes a way to program the agent

Sellers in this new buyer-centric world will be asking us buyers for our preferences – what we like, what we need, what we want – but they will also be asking us what we stand for in terms of more profound values and attitudes. Of course we will not be able to give complete answers to every seller individually.

We will have to use technology to help us: we will have to program our own agent, intelligent but also emotional, to help us out. There are a number of these emotional–intelligent agents around already, but they all ask for your input. And the input is basically to answer the same question as we buyers sometimes pose to good brands – what do you stand for?

Most of these agents will be on the internet, working on our behalf, surfing and searching actively, and filtering and selecting. Some agents will be people assigned by us, to make selections and come up with solutions that fit our demands. They will also need an idea what kind of person we are, what kind of offer would be suitable.

Our vision is of course that the Brand Me Method should become the accepted formula for doing this 'programming' of agents, both real-life and virtual. What's needed is a simple and down-to-earth tool, in the form of a dynamic 'questionnaire', just like Brand Me, that produces the code needed for the agent and in their turn also for the seller, who wants to know who might be interested in their offering and would constitute a perfect match for their brand.

We feel that the toolbox for this is very much in this book. You just have to apply it whenever you enter a situation when someone representing you in the marketplace asks you the key question: 'What do you stand for?' The answer is naturally your own Brand Me Code.

The attitude could be as described in the following general Brand Me Mind Space. This is what we want from sellers in the future. Your own Brand Me Mind Space will be much more specific, of course, and your own only!

The attitude of the Buyer Brand Me

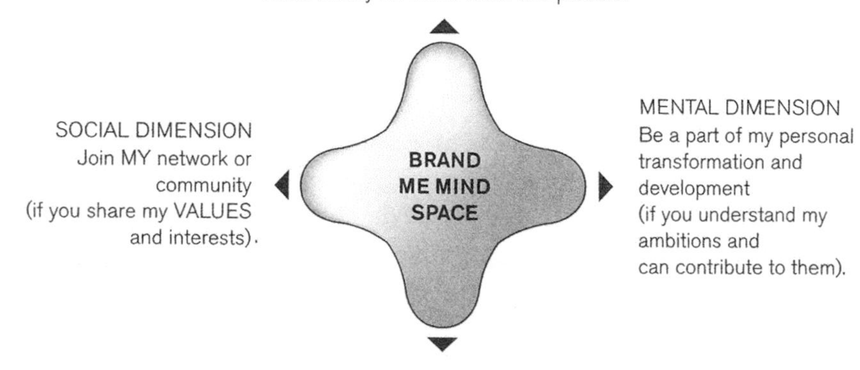
FUNCTIONAL DIMENSION
Don't waste my time.
Remember who I am.
Customize your products and services for me.
Make it easy for me to order and procure.
SOCIAL DIMENSION
Join MY network or community (if you share my VALUES and interests).
BRAND ME MIND SPACE
MENTAL DIMENSION
Be a part of my personal transformation and development (if you understand my ambitions and can contribute to them).
SPIRITUAL DIMENSION
Be my value agent for local or global responsibility within issues of the environment, ecology, ethics, etc. (provided your VALUES and your agenda match mine).

12

chapter twelve

real Brand Me – you are one of a kind

The latest achievement of science is the recent mapping of the complete DNA code. This has long been a dream for scientists. At least as far back as the days of Rousseau – probably earlier but it was with Rousseau that the idea was formulated clearly – the notion has existed that there must be a code governing why everything in nature has turned out to be the way it has. For a very long time science couldn't tell if this was really the case because there were a lot of unknown circumstances.

But now it's going to be possible to take a simple blood test and analyze almost everything about a human body – its built-in dispositions to different illnesses is one interesting area, with the implication that treatment for a lot of common illnesses can be much more prophylactic than ever before.

The growing importance of being special

Another thing that's also going to be possible is to 'manufacture' a copy of your body, a true body double. Some people naively think that this can be prohibited through legislation, but such an interesting possibility will be hard to resist. It realizes a dream for mankind, to produce clones of our favourite heroes in different areas, maybe crossing them and producing super-athletes with the master brains of the world's best chess player. Books and films have toyed with this idea for centuries.

Science fiction that is now (or at least very soon will be) no longer fiction, but pure and real science.

What does this mean for our ideas of being physically different from everybody else on the planet?

The 100,000 possibilities that we now know to be offered by DNA, nature's game of differentiation, makes the idea of a possible differentiation statistically very probable. Or at least a slight differentiation: we also know that we share some 99.5 % of the gene code, with all humans.

Well, the idea that it could be possible to clone every one of us and that it will be totally possible to 'design' a human being means that man can for the very first time have complete control over the process of genetic selection. We can already save and keep in the gene pool those individuals who would otherwise be eliminated from selection by diseases or illnesses or accidents caused by individual character traits.

Alfred Nobel

Sweden has produced a number of very competent business personalities, leaders of both large Swedish and foreign corporations. These include Axel Wennergren (Electrolux) , the Wallenberg family, Per Gyllenhammar (Volvo), Ingvar Kamprad (IKEA), Percy Barnevik (ABB), Hans and Gad Rausing (TetraPak), Erling and Stefan Persson (H&M), and many more, some better known than others, their companies usually being stronger international brands than they themselves personally.

Most of these people have a rather one-dimensional position in our minds, if they are there at all, being built on their Functional Dimensions or maybe the Social. The exception is Alfred Nobel: his personal brand has undoubtedly long-lasting qualities, and the Mind Space he has created in the minds of almost every international audience is considerable.

The difference between Nobel and many other business leaders was his multidimensional personality and ability to communicate it, primarily by the founding of the Nobel Prize.

As an inventor and businessman he was well respected and without doubt created a benefit to the world through his invention of dynamite, the new way to safely handle and use the explosive nitroglycerine. While he made a fortune out of this invention, he also came to have doubts about the effect more efficient explosives might have on world peace.

He was able to put the immediate user benefits into a larger picture, and it was this that generated his feeling that he had to take responsibility for his invention and do something to compensate for its negative effects. That something turned out to be the foundation of the Nobel Prize, which was first of all a peace prize and also a prize for developments within science and medicine.

Alfred Nobel Brand Me Mind Space

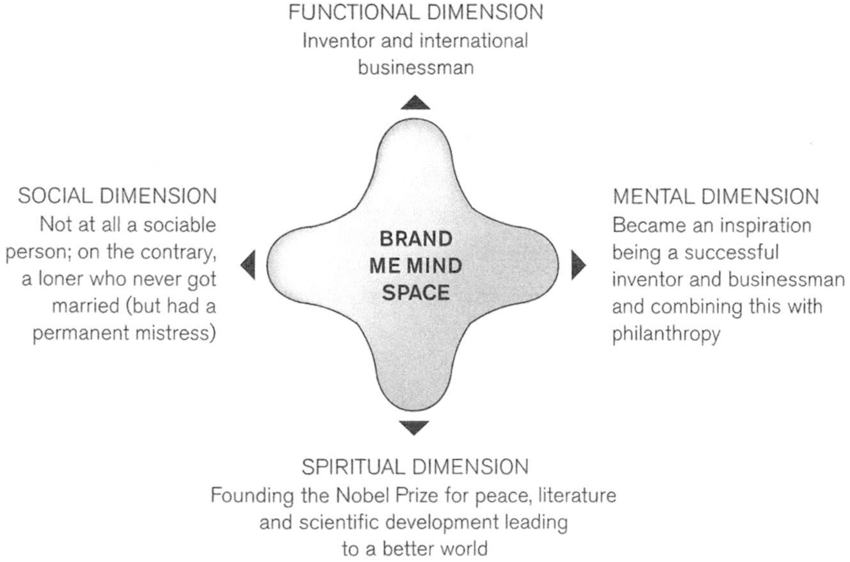

FUNCTIONAL DIMENSION
Inventor and international businessman

SOCIAL DIMENSION
Not at all a sociable person; on the contrary, a loner who never got married (but had a permanent mistress)

BRAND ME MIND SPACE

MENTAL DIMENSION
Became an inspiration being a successful inventor and businessman and combining this with philanthropy

SPIRITUAL DIMENSION
Founding the Nobel Prize for peace, literature and scientific development leading to a better world

Nobel became an inspiration for many through his success as an inventor and businessman combined with his interest in philosophy, literature, science, medicine and technology; he was a truly multidimensional personality. He had a genuine interest in literature and was himself an author, though unpublished during his lifetime.

Alfred Nobel was not at all a sociable person, partly because he was chronically ill for most of his life. On the contrary he was a loner who never got married (but had a permanent mistress). The social life he had was entirely linked to his business and his philanthropy.

But what science has done, setting aside the moral and ethical implications, is going to lead to a strong promotion of the very antithesis of science: the belief in, and a totally new importance of, the concept of an immortal soul. With its new weapon, the cracking of the complete genetic code, science is shooting itself in the foot.

Or, to play with words:

the soul becomes the sole way for a human being to be sure of making a difference.

Maybe the interest in esoteric matters that has lately become more and more prevalent among wider audiences in Western society is a subconscious preparation for this situation. Or is it just a handy coincidence?

The more of nature's mysteries that are unveiled by science, the more naked and exposed conscious human life stands out, with less and less to be discovered. The interest moves, so to speak, to the domain of mankind's psychology. Here no one knows for sure, which is always a great comfort: absolute knowledge is far less fascinating than a good guess.

Our view on this is that firm knowledge in the area of genetics will change a lot about the way we look at ourselves. The Brand Me of tomorrow will be more important. 'Who am I?' will not be a very exciting genetic question any more, but a challenge to establish within yourself a feeling of being different.

It will also mean that intuition, relying on your subconscious mind, will make the whole landscape of self-realization more demanding, more important, but also more interesting. The practical, materialistic and Functional Dimension have been overly important in the last 200–300 years. Other dimensions will now come to the fore, not least the opposite of the Functional Dimension in the 4-D Brand Me Mind Space, the Spiritual Dimension.

What positive lessons can illnesses teach us?

The new science of genetics can tell us a lot about our disposition for illnesses before they have hurt us. Medical science in general has already for years and years been able to tell us a lot about the circumstances under which an illness is likely to break out. And yet almost all of us have friends or relatives who have all the prerequisites for an illness, but haven't suffered from it. And likewise we all know someone who by every available indication shouldn't have been prone to a certain illness but has got it anyway.

Intuitively we have all explained this by reference to the effects of psychology. If an individual has had a positive life, a lot of fun, been passionate about something, or someone, been motivated by work or private life, then we know how to explain why this individual, against all odds, has been able to 'fight' the disease to which he or she by reason of genetics or environment, or both, should be prone. This is of course another important reason to read this book: to pick up one or two pieces of advice to make life richer, better, more motivating and fun, so that one can resist potential illnesses.

Now, what can we learn from this intuitive feeling (which is also backed by the small amount of empirical research that has been done in this area) that health has a psychological background?

To what extent can you change your body with your mind?

Until now this book has been about how mind can change mind. Now it's time to introduce the idea of how mind can actually change body, supported by our intuitive feeling (which is also partly borne out by research) that the mind can override the predispositions for illness in a body.

What does this idea really imply? Well, to start with it implies that we might be able to effect physical change ourselves, using our own mind power.

Instead of using the knife to try to restore and change their looks, a woman, or a man, might be able to use the mind instead!

And here we don't just mean things like 'beauty is in the eyes of the beholder anyway'. We are talking about the ability to actually stop or even reverse the ageing process.

Some of you may think these are very superficial things and not really important: why not accept one's age and one's looks? And of course you are totally right. But the fact that cosmetic surgery is such a big business shows that many people do care about their appearance. Besides, more importantly, a lot of unnecessary energy goes into handling all these problems in people's minds, when they could be using that energy instead to really make a difference, for themselves and for mankind generally.

How much of so-called reality can you change with your mind?

Or rather, how can you explain how these things are happening? because they do all the time. Some individuals do actually change themselves and their physical life with mental powers.

Well, the explanation, and most of us need that, before actually putting this proven tool to work, is generally speaking about **energy**. Energy is the smallest unifying building block in the universe, existing in everything. Our whole existence is about energy changing forms; it also carries messages.

Invisible communication was hard to believe in during the 18th century. At the end of the 19th, Marconi was experimenting with radio transmissions from a boat in the English Channel to an office in London, but even then people thought he was making fun of them. Today with mobile phones in the hands of so many people all around the world, it has become easier to believe that we have the ability as humans to make more universal use of radio waves and their energies. Still there are a lot of effects of energy we haven't started to make practical use of, at least officially, for example telepathy.

What if thoughts were also energy?

When you think about it what else could they be? They are probably waves of energy of a nature that we are not yet able to measure.

If this were true, we could explain how you are able, as we know you are, to change other people's perception of yourself by thinking about the change itself. You can decide for yourself to emit a preferred image or idea, and even a response to it.

Intuition and emotional intelligence are already becoming more important to you. Your challenge now is to fine-tune your senses and to dare to rely on them.

You have to pay more respect to thoughts like: 'I have a feeling ...' or 'I understand things without having the knowledge'.

A conclusion for the future is: you actually may have a sixth sense. And that real change takes place in the subconscious mind. Real difference is subconscious: it's not the visible difference that is most important.

The 'body' and 'soul' of the Brand Me Code

How does your Brand Me Code fit into these ideas?

The left-hand side of the Brand Me Code, where Benefit, Positioning and Style are situated, is the more practical and functional side (it is also very much aligned with the Functional Dimension in the Brand Me Mind Space). Here you have established all the deliverables in terms of how you can be useful to others and how you can be different from others. Style is very much the 'body' of your persona.

On the right-hand side of the Brand Me Code you have all that is very much the 'soul' of yourself, your Mission, your Vision – and of course your Values. All this is less practical and more idealistic (it is also much more aligned with the Spiritual Dimension in your Brand Me Mind Space).

One side is not more important than the other. We need to be both body and soul in our lives.

To have Vision and Values alone, the ideas of a Mission, would achieve nothing without a body to deliver them into daily life. But the 'soul' of your Brand Me Code, like the soul in your life, has to be in charge. Never become a slave to your physical aspect.

A true holistic view, a balance between body and soul, is the true way forward, and your Motto should reflect this. Try to make it as balanced as possible between soul and body, between Idea and Action.

Imagine you had another life …

If asked how we would live another life, most of us would answer 'The same way I have lived this one'. And that is a positive answer it means that you have developed yourself and are basically happy with your life.

But play with your mind for a second: if *in addition to* your current life, which you have used to live out all the things this book has inspired you to do, you could get another one, what would this additional life be like? What knowledge would you take with you?

Five keys to the future

- Timing – the right things at the right time.
- Transparency – everything is open and boundless.
- Telepathy – communication in a refined way.
- Transformation – always developing, always in change.
- Totality – you are one with the universe.

further reading

Branding

Thomas Gad, *4-D Branding*, London: Pearson Education, 2001

NLP

Steve Andreas and Charles Faulkner, *NLP – The New Technology of Achievement*, London: Nicholas Brealey Publishing Limited, 1996

Richard Bandler, *Using Your Brain – For a Change*, Moab, Utah: Real People Press, 1985

Richard Bandler and John Grinder, *Frogs into Princes*, Moab, Utah: Real People Press, 1979

Script writing

Syd Field, *The Screenwriter's Workbook*, New York: Dell Publishing Company, 1998

momentum prescription – Let Us Help You Work Out Which Book Will Suit Your Symptoms

Feel stuck in a rut? Something wrong and need help doing something about it?

- If you need tools to help making changes in your life: **coach yourself** (a good general guide to change)
- If you are considering dramatic career change: **snap, crackle or stop**
- If you need to work out what you'd like to be doing and how to get there: **be your own career consultant**
- If you need help making things happen and tackling the 'system' at work/in life: **change activist**

Feel that you can never make decisions and you just let things 'happen'?

- If you need help making choices: **the big difference**
- If you want to feel empowered and start making things happen for yourself: **change activist**

Feel life is too complicated and overwhelming?

- If you need help working through office politics and complexity: **clued up**
- If you need a kick up the backside to get out of your commerce-induced coma: **change activist**
- If you need an amusing and very helpful modern life survival guide: **innervation**
- If you never have enough time or energy to get things done or think properly: **mental space**

Feel like you might be in the wrong job?

- If you want help finding your destiny job and inspiration to make that dramatic career change: **snap, crackle or stop**
- If you feel like you aren't doing a job that is really 'what you are about': **soultrader**
- If you are struggling with the 'do something worthwhile OR make money dilemma': **change activist**

Feel that you're not the person/leader you should be?

- If you want to be the kind of person others want to follow: **lead yourself**
- If you need help becoming the person you've always wanted to be: **reinvent yourself**
- If you want to work out everything you've got to offer, and how to improve that: **grow your personal capital**

Feel you need help getting your ideas into action?

- If the problem is mainly other people, lack of time and the messiness of life: **clued up**
- If the problem is communicating your thinking: **hey you!**
- If the problem is more ideas than time and you are a bit overwhelmed with work: **mental space**
- If the problem is making change in your life: **coach yourself**

Feel you aren't projecting yourself and managing your career as well as you should?

- If you'd like to be the kind of person people think of first: **managing brand me**
- If you'd like people to listen to your ideas more readily: **hey you!**
- If you'd like to come across as the person you really are inside: **soultrader**
- If you need general help in changing the way you work/life: **coach yourself**
- If you need help working out what you've got and how best to use it: **float you**

Feel you'd like to be much more creative and a real 'ideas person'

- If you need inspiration on how to be innovative and think creatively: **innervation**
- If you need help spreading your ideas and engendering support: **hey you!**